Florence M. Warren.
January 1937

By Pearl S. Buck

FIGHTING ANGEL

THE EXILE

A HOUSE DIVIDED

THE MOTHER

THE FIRST WIFE
AND OTHER STORIES

SONS

THE GOOD EARTH

EAST WIND: WEST WIND

• • •

ALL MEN ARE BROTHERS
[SHUI HU CHUAN]
TRANSLATED FROM THE CHINESE

FIGHTING ANGEL

PORTRAIT OF A SOUL

FIGHTING ANGEL, *the biography of the author's father, is a companion volume to* THE EXILE, *which is a biography of her mother. Together they form a work to be entitled* THE SPIRIT AND THE FLESH

FIGHTING ANGEL

PORTRAIT OF A SOUL

by

Pearl S. Buck

a JOHN DAY book

REYNAL & HITCHCOCK

NEW YORK

Published by

JOHN DAY

in association with

REYNAL & HITCHCOCK

PRINTED AND BOUND IN THE UNITED STATES OF AMERICA
BY THE HADDON CRAFTSMEN, INC., CAMDEN, N. J.

ANGEL—one of an order of spiritual beings, attendants and messengers of God, usually spoken of as employed by him in ordering the affairs of the universe, and particularly of mankind. They are commonly regarded as bodiless intelligences.

—*Century Dictionary.*

"Who maketh his angels spirits
And his ministers a flame of fire."

—*The Epistle to the Hebrews.*

I

YOU might have seen him walking along the street of any little Chinese village or market town, a tall, slender, slightly stooping American. At one time in his life he wore Chinese clothes. I have a picture of him thus, seated upon a stiff carved Chinese chair, his large American feet planted before him in huge Chinese shoes, those shoes which made the Chinese women laugh behind their hands when they cut the soles, and which made many a passerby stop and stare as he strode by in dust or upon cobblestones. He even smiled himself, a little painfully, when open jokes were shouted as he passed. But the Chinese shoes, the long Chinese robe, the little round black Chinese hat with its red button—none of these made him in the least Chinese. No one could possibly mistake him. The spare, big-boned frame, the big, thin delicate hands, the nobly shaped head with its large features, the big nose, the jutting lower jaw, the extraordinary, pellucid, child-blue eyes, the reddish fair skin and slightly curly dark hair—these were purely and simply American.

But he wandered about China for more than half a century. He went there young, and there he died, an old man, his hair snow white, but his eyes still child-blue. In those days of his old age I said to him, "I wish you would write down what your life has been for us to read." For he had traveled the country north and south, east and west, in city and country. He had had adventures enough to fill books and had been in danger of his life again and again. He had seen the Chinese people as few white men ever have—in the most intimate moments of their own lives, in their homes, at marriage feasts, in sickness and in death. He had seen them as a nation in the cycle of their times—he had seen the reign of emperors and the fall of empire, revolution and the rise of a republic and revolution again.

So he wrote down the story of his life as it seemed to him when he was seventy years old. He spent his spare time throughout a whole summer writing it. I used to hear his old typewriter tapping uncertainly during hot afternoon hours when everybody else was sleeping, or in the early dawn, because, having had as a boy to rise early on a farm in West Virginia, he could never sleep late. It was more than a physical inability—it was spiritual. "Arise, my soul, for it is day! The night cometh when no man can work." The night—the night! He remembered always the shortness of life. "As for man, his days are as grass: as a flower of the field, so he flourisheth. For the wind passeth over it, and it is gone; and the place thereof shall know it no more."

But when it was finished the story of all his years made

only twenty-five pages. Into twenty-five pages he had put all that seemed important to him of his life. I read it through in an hour. It was the story of his soul, his unchanging soul. Once he mentioned the fact of his marriage to Carie, his wife. Once he listed the children he had had with her, but in the listing he forgot entirely a little son who lived to be five years old and who was Carie's favorite child, and he made no comment on any of them.

But the omission told as much as anything. For indeed the story was the story not of man or woman or child but of one soul and its march through time to its appointed end. For this soul there was birth, predestined, a duty to be done and it was done, and there was heaven at the end—that was the whole story. There was nothing of the lives of people in it, no merriment of feasts, no joy of love, no tales of death. There was not one word of any of the incredible dangers through which he had often passed. There was nothing in it of empire or emperors or revolutions or of all the stir of changing human times. There was no reflection upon the minds and manners of men or any subtlety of philosophies. The tale was told as simply as the sun rises out of dawn, marches swiftly across the firmament, to set in its own glory.

So others told me his story—his brothers and sisters, Carie, and his son. I heard the talk of people among whom he lived and worked. Most of all, I knew him myself as one among my earliest memories, as one in whose house I spent my childhood, as one who in the last ten years of his life came and lived with me under my roof, and looked to me for care and comfort in his age. In spite of this, for years after he died I could not see what he was. His outlines remained ghostly to me, even when he ate at my table, most of all when he was ill and I tended him. It was only when I came back to the country that had made him and sent him forth that I saw him clear at last. For he was born in America, and he was the child of generations of Americans. No country except America could have produced him exactly as he was.

I do not know the old and precise history of his family and I have not asked because it does not matter. Some time before the American Revolution they came from somewhere in Germany, for the sake of religious freedom. I do not know just when except that I know it was in time for one of his ancestors to be a courier to George Washington, and for two others to fight loyally under Washington's command. I say it does not matter because it is not as an individual that he is significant. If his life has any meaning for others than himself it is as a manifestation of a certain spirit in his country and his time. For he was a spirit, and a spirit made by that blind certainty, that pure intolerance, that zeal for mission, that contempt of man and earth, that high confidence in heaven, which our forefathers bequeathed to us.

The first words which he remembered spoken were words which he never forgot so long as he lived. They remained not so much words as wounds, unhealed. He could not have been more than seven years old. It was a summer's day, in June, a beautiful day, and the afternoon was clear and warm. He was sitting on the steps of the porch of the big farmhouse that was his home. He had been in the orchard looking for a sweet June apple, when he heard the sound of wheels, and looking through the trees he saw a stout, kind neighbor woman coming to visit his mother.

He had always liked Mrs. Pettibrew. He liked her easy cheerful flow of talk, larded with stories, and her rich sudden gusts of laughter, although he was desperately shy, and never answered her questions with more than a smile, strained from him against his will. But he wanted to be near her because she liked everybody and was always jolly. So he had waited until she was seated on the porch and his mother had brought the baby out in her arms and settled herself in the rocking chair to nurse him. Then he sidled around the house and sat very quietly, listening to them, munching his apple. He would not appear interested in them, for after all they were women.

"Howdy, Andy!" Mrs. Pettibrew shouted.

"Howdy," he whispered, his eyes downcast.

"Speak out, Andrew!" his mother ordered him.

They both looked at him. He felt hot all over. He knew, because his older brothers and sisters often told him, that his face easily went as red as cockscomb. He could not have spoken if he would—his mouth was so dry. The apple he had bitten was like dust upon his tongue. He scuffed his bony big toe in the grass miserably. The two women stared at him.

His mother said, worrying, "I declare, I don't know what makes the boy so scary."

"He don't hardly seem like yours, Deborah," Mrs. Pettibrew said solemnly. "He don't even look like yours. I don't know where he gets those light eyes and that red hair. Hiram especially is as handsome a boy as ever I saw —but all your nine children are big and handsome and a sight for sore eyes, except Andy. But then—most families have a runt in 'em."

And this was kind Mrs. Pettibrew! His heart began swelling in him like a balloon. It would burst and he would begin to cry. He wanted to run away and he could not. He sat, his mouth full of dry apple, scuffing his toe back and forth in the grass, caught in agony. His mother released him. She said, kindly enough, "Well, he isn't so handsome, maybe, but he's awfully good, Andy is. None of the others is as good as he is. I always say likely he'll be a preacher, too, like Dave is and like Isaac talks to be —and if he is, he'll be the best of them."

"Well, of course it's better to be good than pretty," Mrs. Pettibrew said heartily. "Say, Deborah, before I forget—I heard a new recipe for quince preserves. . . ."

They forgot him. He could get up now and walk away. The tightness about his heart loosened a little and he could breathe again. He could walk away pretending he had not heard. They went on talking about the quinces, not knowing any more than he did what they had done. They had, that June day, in a farmhouse in the West Virginia hills, set his feet on the path that was to lead him across plains and seas to a foreign country, to spend his years there, to lie at last in a distant grave, his body dust in foreign earth, because his face was not beautiful. All his life he was good. It was better to be good than pretty. "For what is a man profited, if he shall gain the whole world, and lose his own soul?" Goodness was best. On that day he made up his mind he would always be good.

But then there was a tradition of goodness in his family. He could remember his grandmother, sitting beside the fire. The family in her youth had come from Pennsylvania to Virginia. They were all Presbyterians, but not she. She had been born and reared a Mennonite, and to the end of her life she wore her little, dark, close-fitting Mennonite bonnet and held to her rigorous Mennonite faith. She had never been to what she called "a pleasuring." Church on the Sabbath, twice, prayer-meeting on Wednesday until she was old, prayers twice every day—this was the routine of the house which she helped to maintain. She sat in the chimney-place, disallowing all other life.

She had, besides religion, a great belief in ghosts. I used to wonder at a strange timidity in Andrew, and even sometimes in my childhood to be a little ashamed of it. It was not that he was in the least a coward when any necessity was concerned. That is, for the sake of his duty he could and did act in complete disregard of his life. No, it was a childlike timidity, a dislike, for instance, of going upstairs alone in the dark, a reluctance to get up in the night to investigate a noise. I have seen him return half a dozen times to see if a door were locked. "I got to thinking about it until I couldn't be sure," he would confess, smiling half shamefaced.

One day, when he was an old man, he dropped the secret unconsciously, for he never consciously revealed himself to anyone. Someone began, half playfully, one evening about the fire, to tell a ghost story. He could not bear it. He got up and went away. Afterwards he told me alone, always with that half-shamed smile, "The old folks used to tell ghost stories at home until I didn't dare to go to bed. But of course I had to. They weren't just stories, either—they said they were true."

The old grandmother believed them. Sitting in her corner, very old, it was impossible for her to discern the cleaving line between flesh and ghost. So many who had been with her in the flesh were changed to eternal spirits. Soon she, too, would be changed. It was nature to believe that spirits came back to places they had known and loved . . . she, too, would come back. The small boy, sitting unobtrusively among his heartier brothers and sisters, listened and never forgot.

But that house was full of belief in spirits. God was a spirit and God was forever in that house. And the Devil was a spirit, and where God was the Devil was also. They were inseparable—enemies, but inseparable. He grew up familiar with them both. Morning and night he sat and heard his father reading from the Bible the story of the war between these two. Year after year his father plodded straight through that story, for it was his boast to read the Bible through every year. Religion—the house was full of it, too. There were seven sons and six of them were ministers. Religion was their meat and their excitement, their mental food and their emotional pleasure. They quarreled over it as men quarrel over politics. Within its confines they made their personal quarrels.

For it was a quarrelsome family, this family. Father and mother were quarrelsome together. The man was a big, domineering, square-jawed landowner. He had a passion for land. He kept them all poor buying more and more land, and he implanted in every son he had such a hatred for the land that not one of them was willing to farm it after him. I remember that Andrew would not even take the slightest interest in any of Carie's gardens. She felt it a hurt, but I knew he could not help it. I saw him an overworked boy, starving for books, hungry for school, loathing the land and tied to it until he was twenty-one. Only at twenty-one was he free, and then he rode away on the horse his father gave to each of his sons when they came to their majority. He rode away to belated college, to retrieve the years which seemed to him wasted. He never took up spade or hoe again, not for flower or vegetable, not even for Carie's garden.

But until they were all twenty-one they had to work under the man on the land, and his wife and his two daughters had to work in the dairies and the kitchen. The father owned a few Negroes, but he disliked owning them. Besides, he had his sons and his daughters. He drove them all, a big, domineering, thundering fellow, reading the Bible aloud to them night and morning, commanding them. "Honor thy father and thy mother"—although it did not matter so much about the mother. He domineered over them all cheerfully enough, for he had a shrewd sense of humor. He domineered over the whole community. He was head of the school board and he chose the teachers for the one-room school, and when they came, he sheltered them in his big unpainted rambling house, where half a dozen extra people could be fed without noticing it. It was at his house the preachers lodged when they came circuit-riding to the little Presbyterian church, for he domineered over the church, too. Sometimes a preacher made him angry with his preaching and twice, at least, he turned Methodist for short periods purely as a matter of discipline to a refractory preacher. Later he was to suffer for introducing this method of revolt. For Deborah, his wife, after one of their violent quarrels, joined the Methodist church and stayed in it. He never forgave her, not only for the revolt but because it deprived him of a tool against the Presbyterians when he needed it. And of his seven Presbyterian sons, one, Christopher, in the madness of his rebellious youth, joined the Methodist church and remained in it, stubborn, obdurate, as all this family were stubborn and obdurate—"the preachingest family in Greenbrier County," a local newspaper reporter called them when he was writing of them half a century later, "with dissenting blood as strong as lye."

When I was sent home to America to college, I made my first acquaintance with them all. They were, most of them, white-haired by that time, an amazing array of tall, passionate, angry men, not one of them under six feet, every one of them with the same shining bright blue eyes and dry humor and intolerant mind. The quarrel between them was as hot as ever, so hot indeed, that it had become a byword in the county, a cause for shame and laughter, and it had all been argued even in the newspapers. The five Presbyterian preachers quarreled among themselves on many matters, for there was endless material for quarreling—over the period of creation in Genesis and the interpretation of the minor prophets and Song of Solomon, and predestination and the second coming of Christ; and failing these, there then could always be quarreling over the division of the land, the sale of the old farmhouse and its ancient handmade furniture, and whether or not Becky's husband was treating her properly. But they always banded together against the Methodist—although Andrew by then had long been waging his own missionary wars. "Poor Chris," they called the Methodist, striving furiously to pity him for his misguidance.

But when I saw "poor Chris" it was hard to pity him. He was a presiding elder in his chosen church, as rabid and intolerant as any of them, and as bitterly sure of his own theology as the sole road to salvation. It added difficulty that he was very successful and that he had no notion of his pitiable condition, and that he was big and confident and completely arrogant. To hear him roar out the Beatitudes on a Sunday morning, hurling them like cannon balls at his congregation, to see his brows beetle over his bright blue eyes as he shouted, "Blessed are the meek . . ." to hear him insist, "Blessed are the poor in spirit . . ." was a thing to hear and see.

Yes, Andrew grew up in an embattled atmosphere, the atmosphere of a militant religion. But he never quite equaled his brothers in looks or assurance. He was tall, but he stooped a little. He had not the others' full prideful gaze. Girls never looked at him as they did at black-haired Hiram, who strummed a guitar and never quite paid back the money he borrowed to go to college, or as they did at cautious John who prudently married early a rich oldish widow and withdrew from the family religious war and went to the state legislature instead, or as they did, for that matter, at any of the others. Girls did not, indeed, look at Andrew at all because he never forgot what Mrs. Pettibrew had said. Those unforgotten words kept him secretly shy all his life. He withdrew further and further into passionate personal religion. But under his shy, remote exterior all the stubborn fire burned. He was no whit behind any of them there. Indeed, he was the hotter in his goodness, because there was no worldliness in him to ease it.

It was not from Andrew that I heard the story of that terrific family. Indeed, I remember only one tale he ever told me of them. Once when I was a very small girl I pressed him for a story, not really hoping for much. Carie was my great source, but she was busy at that moment with a new baby. Andrew had come in from an evangelistic trip, and in a moment of unwonted ease, he took me on his knee before the fire. It was a knee, I remember, a little bony beneath my short skirts, for he was always spare, having great scorn for anyone who was fat. If a fellow missionary developed a paunch Andrew was at once indignant and suspicious of him—"He's eating too much," he would exclaim, "he's getting lazy." It was the great indictment, next to an unsound theology. On this occasion, perched upon his ridgy knee, I inquired, "Do you know just one story?" I stared into his very clear, not unkindly eyes. "Not one out of the Bible," I amended hastily. "I know all those." He was taken aback—clearly he had been raking over the Old Testament in his mind. "Let me see," he said, ruminating. "Maybe when you were a little boy?" I suggested, to be helpful. I waited for what seemed a long time. He could not, apparently, remember much about having been a little boy. But at last he thought of something.

"Once my father had some pigs," he began solemnly, remembering, staring into the fire, "and those pigs would keep squeezing through the fence of the orchard where they were supposed to stay to eat the windfalls. They kept getting into the front yard. Well, my father was a short-tempered man. He grew very angry. He'd rush out and chase them back no matter what he was doing, but pretty soon they'd be in again. One day he got so angry he couldn't stand it. He raced after them clear to the fence and they ran as hard as they could and squeezed in just ahead of him—that is, all but one. The last one was fatter than the others and he stuck. My father whipped out his pocket-knife and cut off his tail."

I stared at Andrew, astonished. "What did he do that for?" I asked.

"Just to teach him a lesson," he answered, smiling a little.

But I remained grave. "What lesson?" I inquired further.

He gave one of his unexpected restrained laughs. "Maybe not to get so fat," he said.

Later I was to hear many tales of that intrepid man, father of Andrew. People feared him and liked him, laughed at him and trusted him. Rampaging and angry, enormously stubborn, he was endlessly kind to his poor neighbors and utterly ruthless to his family. Once he went around the corner of one of his big barns and discovered a poverty-stricken fellow standing by a knot-hole, holding a large sack into which was pouring a steady stream of wheat. When he saw Andrew's father, he ran. Andrew's father said nothing at all. He took the man's place, and stood holding the bag, his eyes twinkling. After a while a voice came from within the barn, "Ain't it about full?"

"It's just about full, I reckon," he answered amiably.

There was dead silence within the barn. He knotted the mouth of the sack and heaved it to his great shoulders and went inside and discovered a cringing, waiting figure.

"There—take it," he said, flinging the sack at the man, recognizing a poor neighbor, a tenant farmer. "Next time come and ask me and I'll give it to you!"

I never saw Andrew's father and mother, but I have their tintypes. His father has a square indomitable face with the most arrogant eyes I have ever seen. Only a man sure of God and of his own soul can have such eyes as those. I have never seen them in other human faces.

But the woman is his match. Her jaw is no whit less strongly turned than his, and if her eyes have not that gleam of God in them, they have the calmness of the Devil. No wonder God and the Devil were such realities in that turbulent home! Someone told me—not Andrew—that when Deborah was sixty years old she not only turned Methodist for good and all, but she decided she had worked enough and that she would never work again. She changed completely with this decision. From being the incessantly busy, capable, managing mother of the big household, turning out cheeses and pies and cakes and loaves of bread, for she was a notable cook, she became a woman of complete leisure. She never so much as made her own bed again. She sat on the wide porch of the farmhouse all day long on pleasant days, rocking placidly, and in bad weather she sat by the sitting-room window that looked out on the road. She took walks by herself, a tall, always slender, upright figure. She went to her Methodist church alone except when Christopher was home.

Her family were amazed, and her husband was almost beside himself with rage. But she lived them all down and for nearly thirty-five years maintained her complete leisure while perforce she was waited upon by one after the other of them. She became a center for the women of the neighborhood to visit. Once, all unplanned, twenty-two women met there to spend the day, and a dozen was nothing uncommon. They sat on the porch or in the sitting-room, gossiping, strengthening one another. If God was preeminent in that house, it was only by a very narrow margin.

But it is Andrew's story I am telling and none of these others matter, because they mattered so little to him. They gave him his body and soul, they kept God and the Devil hot about him, and it is true that in certain large ways they shaped him. He learned his creed from them, the creed not only of his theology but of his place in creation as a man. In that house bursting with its seven great sons, roaring with the thunder of the quarrel between man and woman, he heard it often shouted aloud that the Bible said man was head of the woman. It had to be shouted often to that indomitable old woman, eternally in her rocking chair. It made no impression on her, but it made a deep impression on her seven sons. Carie told me once that of those seven great boys, grown young men when she first saw them, not one would have thought of going upstairs to bed unless one of the two sisters lighted a candle and went ahead of them, one after the other. What a procession it was—David, Isaac, Hiram, John, Christopher, Andrew and Franklin! And the sisters were Rebecca and Mary, tall women as their brothers were tall, subdued, smoldering, forbidden by their father to marry in their youth because he and his sons had need of their services, marrying at late last men too humble for them. Of this furious seed, out of this turbulent soil, Andrew was born.

II

THE story should begin when Andrew left home at twenty-one, because Andrew himself always began his life there, counting as worthless the years when he had to do nothing but the labor of his hands to feed nothing but human bodies. And no one seems to remember much about him as a child or a boy. Somebody said once, an old woman who had been a neighbor for a while, "That boy always had the hands of an old man—they said he was born with old hands." And there is only one thing to be told of his adolescence, because that is all I really know, except that I heard rumors of a subdued puckish humor in him, a sort of humor which indeed he kept all his life. I used to think it tinged with cruelty sometimes, although I am sure it was not meant to be so. But I met once an old man who knew him as a child, who went to the one-room school with him in the few winter months when they were not busy on the big farm. The old man spat tobacco juice and grinned when he told it. "That Andrew!" he observed. "When he was a boy he could make a face fit to bust a cat open with laughin' at him. Then when we was all hollerin' and snickerin' the teacher'd turn around mad and he'd be the only one with a sober face." Whatever the humor was, it was always firmly repressed behind a sober face and it leaked out only in dry jokes and occasional barbed thrusts. It never rollicked or burst out full and free, and because he so held it back, there was often bitterness in his joke, and his laughter was silent or at most a single "haw!" of sound.

Once I said to him, "What did you do all those years of your youth?"

His face shadowed. "I worked for my father," he answered briefly.

His sister Mary said to me once, "Pa wanted Andrew to stay on the place because he was so reliable. He was the one boy out of the lot that you could be sure would get every chore done on time and as it ought to be done. He had an awful sense of duty."

"I suppose you know he hated every bit of it," I said.

"That didn't make any difference to him," she answered vigorously. She smiled. "Nor to Pa," she added.

She was an old woman then, too fat, coarse, a little sloppy. Years of living with a man beneath her had made her careless. But when she smiled one saw the family eyes, hard, fearless, blue.

Yet those years of his early adolescence were tremendous years, for they were the years of the Civil War. Four of the sons went to fight the North. David, Hiram, Isaac, John—they marched out of the house in grey uniforms, transferring for a brief while their war against the Devil to the Yankees. Two were wounded, one was kept prisoner for a long time in a Northern prison. I never heard Andrew mention any of it except to say one day that he had disliked bean soup ever since Isaac had come back from the war and told them he had to eat it three times a day in the Yankee prison. "At that," Andrew added with his wry smile, "it was so thin Isaac said he had to dive for the beans." And when the youngest and last of his children went to tell Andrew of her betrothal, he looked up from his page long enough to say with that wry look of his, "I don't know what I've done to have all three of my children marry Yankees!" Yes, there was one other memory in him—he never heard the name of Abraham Lincoln mentioned without commenting drily, always in the same words, "Lincoln was a very much over-rated man." In Andrew's house I grew up never knowing that Lincoln was a national hero, or that across the sea in America children had a holiday from school on his birthday.

But wars and the times of men were of no importance in the life of Andrew. Somewhere in those adolescent years while he served his father carefully in silence and in hated waiting, he received his missionary call. I know, because that brief story he wrote of his life begins with it. So far as he was concerned here was the dawn of his life, his real birth. "At the age of sixteen," he wrote, "I received the first intimation of Divine Call to the mission field."

Afterwards, questioning him, I pieced out the story from his scanty words. It was, of course, inevitable that he should be a preacher of the gospel. It is impossible to think of any of those tall men as ministers—they were all preachers, not ministers, and so was Andrew. I suppose it was inevitable that all of them should be preachers. There were reasons for it, aside from the opportunity it gave them to exercise personal authority over other people's minds and lives. At that time it was a calling of high social position. The preacher in a community was also the leader in other ways, and an ambitious young man wanting power could scarcely find a more satisfactory way of getting it. And these seven young men were all ambitious and power-loving.

But I have it from Andrew himself that at first he never thought of being a missionary, or indeed of leaving his home state. He had, in his curious mixture, a clinging love of home. I think it was really a part of his sense of physical timidity that made him love security and safety and shelter. If he had not been born in a religious age, he would have been a scholar, shutting himself into some warm book-lined room for life. I have seen him come back from a long hard journey on foot or donkey-back through half a Chinese province, and be almost childishly comforted with food and a cup of hot tea and a blazing fire. "It's good to be home—oh, but it's good to be home!" he would murmur to himself.

"I never left home without an inner struggle," he told me when he was an old man. But he was born with a restless, angry conscience, and I never knew him to postpone the hour of his going or shirk the most difficult or dangerous journey. He carried his scourge in his own heart. And because he was so rigorous with himself, he was unmerciful in his judgment upon lesser men. I have heard him exclaim against a fellow missionary, "He doesn't like to leave the comforts of his home—he's lazy!" If he had never been tempted himself, or if being tempted he had sometimes yielded, he might have been gentler with his fellows. But he was invincible toward weakness, as all are who are strong enough for their own temptations. For he was strong enough for the greatest conflict of his life—the conflict of his sense of duty with his strange physical timidity.

This is the story of his call. A missionary from China came to preach in the Old Stone Church in Lewisburg, West Virginia, and he told the tale of his life. Andrew, then sixteen, sat in the line of his family in the front pew, listening to the story of hazard and danger and desperate human need, and listening, he was afraid. He was so afraid that he hurried home alone, and avoided the missionary. But his father brought the tall gaunt man home to the big Sunday dinner, and there he could not be avoided. And the missionary, looking down the long line of sons, said to his father, "Out of all these sons you have begotten, will you not give one to China?"

No one answered. The father was taken aback. It was all very well to go to hear a missionary once a year or so and give him a square meal afterwards and drive him in the surrey to his next church, but it was quite another thing to give him a son.

"I don't want the boys to get such notions," Deborah said decidedly from her end of the table.

"God calls," the missionary said quietly.

"Have some more chicken and gravy," the father said hastily. "Here, Deborah—more mashed potatoes—fetch the hot bread, Becky—eat, man! We're hearty folk around here!"

Nobody answered, but terror caught Andrew's heart. Suppose God should call him to go? The food turned dry in his mouth.

Afterwards he went for days weak with terror. "I believe I lost ten pounds," he said, remembering after fifty years. He grew afraid to say his prayers lest God should call him as he prayed. He tried not to be alone lest heaven crack and God's voice come down to him, commanding him. He never felt home so warm, so sheltering. Yet he was miserable. "I was avoiding God," he wrote when he was an old man. "I knew it, and I was miserable."

For it was a necessity to his being that he feel the

channel clear between him and his God, and now, do what he would and go where he would, he felt the pursuit of God.

His mother laid hold of him one day. "What's wrong with you, Andy? You look like you're getting the jaundice!"

For a long time he would not tell her, but she clutched him firmly by the shoulder. She was still taller than he was. Finally he mumbled the truth, his eyes filling with helpless tears. "I'm afraid I'm going to get the call," he said.

"What call?" she asked. She had entirely forgotten the missionary.

"To the foreign field."

"Get out!" she said with vigor. "Your pa wouldn't hear to it! He's counting on you to take hold of the land."

I suppose nothing would infuriate Andrew more, though he has been long dead, than to know that this had anything to do with making God's call more tolerable. But certainly his soul revolted at his mother's words. He wrenched his shoulder loose from her and strode off. He would never stay on the land, call or no call. Anger swept out fear, for the moment. He went away into the woods alone and there he cried out resolutely to God. "I subdued my stubborn heart," he wrote. "I cried out to God, 'Here am I—send me!' Immediately peace filled my soul. I was afraid no more. I felt myself strong. When I gave up my own will, God's power descended upon me. And God sent me."

So his life was decided. But he said nothing then. He planned his years. Five years more he must serve his father. He knew, because of the other sons ahead of him, that on his twenty-first birthday his father would give him the choice he had given each of the others, to stay at home and receive wages for the work he had until then been doing for nothing, or to receive a good horse and a hundred dollars and ride away. They had all chosen to ride away and so would he. He would tell no one, but he would ride away and go to college and to seminary and fit himself for his life. His heart beat at the thought. Books—there would at last be plenty of books. He was always starved for them, and he never had enough of school. One of the few fervent things I ever heard him say was, "I *loved* school!" Indeed, I do not believe I ever heard him use the word "love" in any other connection with himself. "God so loved the world . . ." that use I heard often enough. It was odd to hear him say, "I love . . ." I remember it, because I was being sent away to school those days, myself, and was not at all sure about loving it, and I had never thought of his loving anything except God.

On his twenty-first birthday he rode away, then, his call hot in his breast. His life was begun and he came to it starved. His story tells me he was not ready for college at once. The Civil War had interrupted all schools, and while the older sons, when they came home again and before they went away, taught the younger children, still he was very unevenly prepared. So he went for a year to Frankfort Academy—I know no more than that—and thence to Washington and Lee University, where Hiram had gone just before him.

My first knowledge of those years was when I was still a little girl. I was rummaging all the book shelves in the mission house on the hill above the Yangtse River, in a state of starvation very much like Andrew's own. All the books in the world would not have been enough for me, and in that mission house there were very, very few of the world's books. So, because Andrew was away on one of his long preaching tours, I did what I never dared to do when he was home—I went into his study to search again his shelves, not very hopefully, for I had combed them before and had read Plutarch's *Lives* and Josephus and Fox's *Martyrs,* and anything at all promising a story. This day I was so desperate I took down Geikie's *Commentary on the Bible*—and put it back again. It was worse than nothing. Then in sheer emptiness I decided to look through the drawers of his old roller-top desk. I remembered having once seen some books there when he chanced to open a drawer. But when I looked they were only his mission account books, kept in meticulous detail in his slightly wavering handwriting, for he had a sunstroke once that nearly ended him, and left him with a right hand that trembled a little when he held it to write. I opened one drawer after the other. In the bottom one I saw a heap of curious rolls of leathery paper. They were very dusty and no one had looked at them for a long time. Indeed, some of them had never been opened. I took them out, one by one, and unrolled them. Upon them were printed Latin words. I was studying Latin by then myself, and I saw his name, and always the three words, *Magna cum laude*.

"What do they mean?" I went to ask Carie.

She was in her bedroom, darning swiftly, a big sock stretched over her hand. Those spare bony feet of his, walking miles every day on their mission, over city stones and cobbled roads and across dusty footpaths, kept her sewing basket always piled high. Pride came over her face like a light. "Your father was graduated from the university with honors in every subject," she said. Years afterwards when I went to college I was inclined to be hurt when he said nothing to a report card which I felt was distinguished by A's. But if he said nothing it was because he expected no less of his child, and indeed, expected something rather better than he ever got from her, I am afraid. I once to my astonishment received a mark of 99 for geometry, a subject in which I was never at my best. "A good mark," he said reservedly and added at once, "a hundred would have been better."

He was desperately poor in college. I can imagine him, tall, already slightly stooped but with the lofty bearing of great dignity which he always had. It was there already, because his fellow students were afraid of him and none of them seemed very near him, and that was to be true of people all his life. He was very nearsighted, too, and did not know it, nor had anyone ever paid enough heed to him to find it out. He sat in the front seat if he could, and when he could not, he copied what was written on the board from one of his fellows. He could not recognize people unless they passed near enough to touch him, and so he never learned to look at faces or to be observant of anything around him and he was driven the further in upon himself. Later when one of his professors suggested glasses his delight was simply that now he could see better to read. He had no social life at the university, partly because he was poor and wanted only to buy more books, and partly because he did not want society. He wanted only to get the meat out of his books. Hiram, the handsome, could go to parties and strum his guitar and call on pretty girls, but Andrew did none of these things. And yet he was tremblingly happy. He got up earlier than ever, with an enormous sense of luxury because there were no cows to be milked, no chores to be done. He could follow his single desire, his books. He would excel them all there. Hiram could never approach him; none of them could, not even David, gifted almost to the point of genius in languages.

I know, for Andrew told me, that he was too poor to afford eleven dollars a month for board in the mess hall, and that he and Hiram lived in one room in the old wooden dormitory, and cut cord wood in winter and stacked it in one corner of their room and cooked scanty meals of mush and potatoes over the same fire that warmed them. He told me this because it seemed to him incredible that a girl could spend so much, forty years later, at college. Listening, she had not the heart to tell him that what he gave her, thinking it generous, was not enough to pay for her food and room, even. She sat silent, and after he was gone, went away and found herself a job of teaching in a night school. But for Andrew the times had not changed. He never lived in time but in eternity.

I know no more of his college life except that he was graduated, bright with honors and warmed with unwonted public attention, and except this one thing, which remained to him a tragedy all his life, even when he was an old man.

The night after his graduation, when he was to leave the next day, a fire broke out in the ramshackle wooden dormitory. Hiram had been graduated a year before. Andrew was alone, and being young and wearied with excitement and triumph, he slept heavily. Only at the last moment was he wakened by thick smoke and a terrible heat. The house was on fire. He fumbled his way to the stairs which were already blazing, and ran down to safety. They collapsed behind him. No one was burned, since nearly everyone was already gone. But he stood watching the flimsy building blaze and dim and drop to ash in such agony as I do believe he never felt again. His books, in which his life was bound, which he had bought so hardly, one by one, were gone.

He went home again, penniless. Everything was the same. His father received him with rough welcome, with scanty well-meaning sympathy. Books! Well, wasn't he done with them? Was he ready to settle down to real work now? Wages were ready. But he was not ready. It seemed impossible to begin again that dull physical round. He dreaded the labor which absorbed the powers of the brain as a useless by-product and left the numb bodily fatigue which could only be assuaged by sleep. He chanced upon an advertisement in a religious paper. "Wanted: A young man to sell Bibles." It struck him at once that to sell Bibles was to do more than merely sell a book—it was to spread wide the word of God. So he answered the advertisement and a package of Bibles arrived and he set out on foot to go from house to house.

"I do not know," he wrote years later in that abridgment of his life, "where the fault lay, but I sold only one copy. Whether the people were very hard of heart or whether I was not fortunate in my address, I do not know. I only know that God did not bless my endeavor."

The truth is of course that anyone less like a salesman than Andrew was never created, and I suppose it takes salesmanship also to sell the Bible. I can imagine him approaching a house in a misery of shyness. I can imagine a hearty housewife opening her door in the early morning in the thick of after-breakfast work to discover a tall, stooped, blushing young man upon her threshold, inarticulately holding forth a book.

"Madam, I am selling Bibles. I do not know—"

"We've got a Bible," she doubtless replied with vigor. After all, of course every house had a Bible. Wasn't it a Christian country? She slammed the door and plunged her hands into the dishpan—a Bible, of all things!

"I concluded at the end of a month," Andrew wrote, "that God had not called me to the task of selling anything."

So he went back to his father, not knowing what else to do, and his father, chuckling a little, paid him generously enough, although to Andrew no pay was enough for work he hated.

All his years at college he had kept secret within himself his determination to be a missionary. And how Andrew could keep his own counsel! He could hold a dear plan inside himself for years and shape every end to it, and everyone to it. Years later this secrecy was a torment to Carie, an exasperation to his fellow missionaries. Andrew had early discovered that the most successful means of doing what he liked was to do it without telling anyone what he was doing. But as the summer wore away it was necessary that he tell his father and mother that he was going to seminary in the autumn to fit himself to be a missionary. He had saved his wages, every penny. In the lavishness of the food upon the table what he ate was never missed. And his brother John had by then married his rich widow and had promised to help him with a loan. David, too, then preaching in a little town in the next county, was sympathetic.

He told his parents, and was instantly met with terrific opposition from his father.

"Tomfoolery!" the stormy old man roared, shaking his shaggy white hair back from his forehead. "Go and preach, if you have to—though I'll say six sons out of seven is what I call too much of a good thing. But to go gallivantin' to foreign countries is beyond any man's call."

"Not beyond God's call," said Andrew. He was by all odds the most stubborn man I ever knew when God called him to a thing. So I know his father's anger and roaring only set him harder in his own way. Whatever his mother might have said, left to herself, no one can tell. But when she heard the old man's verdict, she was immediately mild out of contrariness.

"I don't care, Andy," she said, rocking back and forth. "You do as you have a mind to—there's only one thing I ask of you as my son. Promise me, Andrew."

In his relief and gratitude he promised her. "I certainly promise, Mother."

He had not dreamed of what her condition would be.

"You shan't go till you find a wife to go with you," she said, rocking to and fro. "I wouldn't be easy if you hadn't a wife to take care of you."

He nearly fainted. A wife! He had not thought of such a thing. He had never dreamed of marrying—a wife, when he had to live in strange dangerous countries—a woman—he didn't know a single one!

"How can I ever find a woman willing to go?" he groaned. "You might as well forbid me to go!"

"Oh, get out," his mother replied amiably. "There's always women willing to marry any two-legged thing in pants."

Andrew went away in a daze. His mother was not reassuring.

In the end it seems he put the matter up to God. I am not saying he did not make a few efforts himself. But they were futile. I do not know about them in any detail, since he always maintained the strictest silence about his failures, whatever they were, and forgot them at once. But one evening when he was a very old man he told me something. In those years I sat a while with him alone every evening, so that he might have someone to talk with if he chose. He talked more in those hours than he ever had before—not consecutive talk, but bits of incidents plucked at random out of three-quarters of a century of life. I had to do my own piecing. He said suddenly on one of those evenings, "You might have had Jennie Husted to be your mother."

"What!" I exclaimed. It was impossible to imagine anyone except Carie for our mother. I instantly resented Jennie Husted. Who was she?

"I worried a lot in seminary because of my promise to my mother," he said, staring into the fire. "I observed many young ladies—from a distance, that is," he added quickly. "If any seemed at all possible, devout and well grounded in faith, I asked them first if they had ever considered the foreign field. It seemed prudent to ascertain their feeling on this point before I took the time and expense of proceeding further. They all replied in the negative."

"But who was Jennie Husted?" I demanded.

"My trial sermon," he proceeded in his calm fashion, disregarding interruption, "was considered very good—in fact, so good that it was published in a church paper. It was entitled, 'The Necessity of Proclaiming the Gospel to the Heathen, with Especial Reference to the Doctrine of Predestination.' After its publication, I received a letter from a Miss Jennie Husted. In it she warmly supported my views and we entered into a correspondence. Her home was in Louisville, Kentucky. In the last year of my seminary course I asked for permission to call upon her. I felt a strong premonition that God had called her to be my wife. I went all that distance to see her, under that impression. But when we met, I found I was mistaken."

"What happened?" I asked, exceedingly curious.

"I was simply mistaken," he repeated firmly, and would say no more.

"Well, at least tell me what she looked like," I pressed, bitterly disappointed.

"I do not remember," he said with great dignity.

I never knew any more than that about it. It did not seem to me, however, that Carie's place as our mother had been seriously threatened.

III

I PUT out of my mind entirely Carie's side of their meeting and their marriage. After all, so far as Andrew was concerned, Carie, as Carie, had very little to do with it anyway. It was providential—that is, God provided it that in the summer of his graduation from seminary when he was ready for service and held back only by his promise to his mother, a young woman should have been found who was interested, or so it appeared, in going as a missionary with him.

He had come to his brother David's house this summer, as he had the summer before, to study under his brother. David was a scholar in Sanskrit, in Hebrew, in Greek, not to mention other biblically important languages. And besides, Andrew acted as supply for neighboring churches as well as for David. It gave him practice, as well as a chance of earning a little money. And Andrew doubtless needed the practice. He could never throw off wholly that shrouding mantle of shyness. A certain secret doubt of himself as a man was always mingled with his certainty of himself as God's messenger. There was never any doubt of his divine guidance, never any doubt of his rightness. I think the truth of it is that he never could get Mrs. Pettibrew's words out of his mind. All his life he rather wistfully admired handsome and clever young men. Many handsome and clever young Chinese certainly did what they liked with him.

Still, in spite of Mrs. Pettibrew, he had turned out better than he knew. The red thatchy hair of his boyhood had miraculously turned a dark curly brown. I know it was an astonishment because the change came rather quickly so that he was teased about having dyed his hair, to his horror. Carie told me that when she first saw him his hair was undeniably red, but the summer he proposed to her, the same summer they were married and went to China, his hair was dark. He was, she said, "Not bad-looking at all." But he kept his sandy eyebrows and his moustache was reddish, and later when he came and went among the Chinese and grew a beard, they called him "red-beard," although those who knew him nicknamed him—for everyone in China has a nickname—"The Fool about Books." Well, he was in love with books always, to the day we buried him with his little Greek New Testament, which was more a part of him than any of us ever were.

I have a picture of him the summer he married Carie. In the fashion of those days, he is seated and she is standing beside him, her hand a little awkwardly upon his shoulder. But obviously he does not know it is there. He looks out of the picture with the gaze I know so well, a gaze compounded of that obstinate jutting jaw, those childlike clear eyes, and a beautiful, saintly brow. That untroubled brow of his remained exactly the same, though he would have been eighty his next birthday had he lived until the year came round again to summer. I never knew which of those three parts of his face were more unchangeable, but I think it was his brow. It was wide and smooth, the skin transparently fair. He wore his sun helmet low over his eyes, so that the reddish-brown sunburn of his cheeks never reached his brow. In the morning, after his habitual hour of prayer alone in his study, it was marked by three strips of flaming red where he had leaned his head upon his outspread fingers. But these soon faded, leaving the smooth high brow white. He was never bald and the dark hair grew thinner and silvery. For he never suffered. He lived that extraordinary and rare thing, a completely happy life, and there was never a line upon that really noble brow.

I put relentlessly aside Carie's side of the story.

In those long evenings of his old age I asked questions of him. "What did Mother look like when you married her?" I asked him. He stared into the coal fire he loved to have burning upon the hearth in his room. He spread his hands to the blaze. They showed no trace of the youth spent upon a farm. They were a scholar's hands, rather large, very thin and finely shaped, the nails meticulously tended. But then I never saw him otherwise than neat and spotlessly clean. Never once in all our shifting poverty-stricken childhood, or in all the later years of his age, did I ever see him except freshly shaven, his stiff wing collar white, his hair brushed. He was fastidious in all his poverty. He would never own more than two suits—if he had more he gave them away to someone who needed clothing—and those suits he wore to threadbareness, but he was always fresh and clean. Wherever he went, traveling and stopping by night in little filthy Chinese inns, he never began the day without bathing himself in some fashion. And I never saw him with dirty hands.

"Your mother?" he reflected. "I don't exactly remember. She had dark hair and eyes and she was fond of singing."

"How did you propose to Mother?" I asked, too boldly.

He was embarrassed. "I wrote her a letter," he replied. He considered for a moment and then added, "It seemed to me to be the only way of putting everything clearly before her for her mature reflection."

"Mother's father didn't want her to marry you, did he?"—this to goad him a little into remembering.

He replied tranquilly. "There was some nonsense, but I wouldn't stand for it. He was a man with a temper, although a good man in his way—but very stubborn. I have little use for stubborn people."

"And then?"

"Well, we were married and came straight to China.

I remember that no one told me about berths on the train and we sat up."

"I thought somebody said you bought only one ticket on the train," I said, prodding him.

"Oh, that," he said, "there was nothing to that."

"You mean it was only a story?"

"Oh, of course I bought another ticket as soon as my attention was called to it," he said.

And he laughed at himself, his dry, half-silent laugh, because he had been such an innocent about tickets and travel. The real joke of it was that he could not realize that he was never anything but an innocent about all worldly affairs. Tickets and the intricacies of travel remained a bewilderment to him, although in some fashion or another he always arrived at his destination. This he did by the simple expedient of invariably being very early at a dock or a station so that if he wandered into the wrong ship or train somebody would find him there and put him off in time for him to discover the right one. He traveled, of course, incredible distances, and by any means he could. Yet we never saw him start on a ship or a train, or indeed in any modern conveyance, without a sense of his helplessness and of anxiety and doubt of his arrival, and what amounted to a certainty that he would never get back again. Yet somehow, usually through the help of some pitying person who perceived his bewilderment, he always came back safely. He had a principle against luxury of any sort, although secretly he loved its comfort, and he would not hear of traveling first-class, nor until he was a very old man, even second-class. When trains began to be built in China he was as excited as a child and took the greatest pleasure in traveling by them over country through which he had once plodded on foot or upon a donkey. But for years he steadfastly refused to ride in any except the third-class, where the benches were narrow boards, and if we did not watch him he would even climb into a fourth-class coolie car. It was not because he was penurious for the sake of money. He was penurious for God's sake, that everything might go into that cause to which he had dedicated his life—and to which also he ruthlessly and unconsciously dedicated all those lives for which he was responsible.

His honeymoon upon a ship crossing the Pacific was spent in improving his knowledge of the Chinese language. He had begun the study months before. He ordered his life now as he always did. A certain number of hours each day were spent in the study of Chinese, a certain number on Hebrew and Greek. His Bible he always read in those languages. The great dissatisfaction of his life was with the inadequate translations of the Bible into English and later into Chinese. For all the absoluteness of his creed he was a thorough scholar, and he never regarded any translation of the Bible as the final Word of God. The final Word of God was there, locked somehow into the Hebrew and Greek originals, and it was the passion of his life to uncover the truth of the Word. The first heresy he ever uttered—and he was full of unconscious heresies which he would never acknowledge as such—was that "they" were all wrong in translating the word "day" in the first chapter of Genesis—it meant not "day" but "period"—"God created the world in seven periods," he used to say. But he put no faith whatever in scientists, in their study of man's beginning—"A lot of old fellows getting excited over a few scratches in some cave or other," he would say, dismissing the lot. And Darwin he relentlessly held to be a soul possessed by Satan. "Evolution!" he would snort. "Devilution, I call it!" Yet he could listen with wistful reverence to some Biblical archaeologist recounting the uncovering of Nineveh or Tyre, and he could hear with amazing humility of belief such fantasies of fulfillments of ancient prophecies, such madness of miracles, such imaginations of resurrection and millenniums as are not to be found between the covers of any of the novels he disdained to read because they were not "true."

Into Chinese, then, he plunged with ardent enjoyment. He was, as a matter of fact, a man of genius in all languages, and he delighted in the intricacies of Chinese, in aspirate and non-aspirate, in tones—ascending, level, level on an ascent, descending, exclamatory—in all the fine shades and distinctions of meaning and constructions. He spoke Chinese as few white men ever do, with feeling and literary precision. It came at last to be more native to him than his own tongue—he spoke it far more. Once in an American pulpit, when he went back on a furlough, he rose before a great audience to pray. As he always did, he stood a long moment in silence, to empty his mind of all except God. Then, feeling no one there except himself and God, he began to pray—and the prayer came in Chinese. Only when he was half through did he realize what he was doing. He stopped and then went on in English. But the prayer became nothing. He was conscious of others there now, and God was gone.

Indeed, few Chinese even spoke as accurately as he did, for few knew the syntax of the language as he did. There exists today a little book he once wrote on Chinese idioms, a really valuable study, written with the compression which was natural to him. And it was characteristic that when it was revised and he was urged to make an index to it, he refused to do it, saying, "It won't hurt people to look for what they are after, if they really want it."

The very precision of his knowledge, however, made his Chinese speech seem too literary, and indeed it was often beyond the comprehension of ordinary people. I remember it was a life-long complaint against Carie that she had a certain carelessness in Chinese pronunciation. "Your mother," he would say to us plaintively, "will never learn that certain words are aspirates." He would beseech her, his sensitive ear offended to agony, "Carie, I beg you, that word is aspirate—"

To which she replied robustly, "What's the odds? I can't be bothered, so long as they understand me. Besides, the common people understand me better than they do you."

It did not help the situation at all that this last remark was perfectly true.

When I look back over the eighty years of Andrew's life, I realize that the pattern of it is very simple. The first twenty-eight years were years of struggle and preparation, carried on doggedly with a very genius of stubborn persistence to that moment when he set sail for China. From that moment, for fifty years the pattern is one of simple happiness. All around me today, in every country of the world, I see people struggling for personal happiness. They struggle in a hundred ways. They put their hopes in a hundred different things—in new forms of government and social theory, in plans for public welfare, in private accumulation of wealth. None is quite free from that search for individual happiness. For however he may disguise his struggles under noble names of causes and crusade, the bitter truth is that no perfectly happy individual takes part in any struggle. Andrew was the happiest person I have ever known and he never struggled. He went his way, serene and confident, secure in the knowledge of his own rightness. I have seen him angry at others because they obstructed that way of the Lord he trod so surely, but I never saw him puzzled or distrustful of himself. I never saw him in undignified argument with others. He took his own way with proud tranquillity. There was a greatness in his clear determination.

Nor can I tolerate for a moment any mawkish notion that it was his religion that filled him with that might. Religion had nothing to do with it. Had he been a lesser mind he would have chosen a lesser god, had he been born for today he would have chosen another god, but whatever he chose would have been as much god to him. Whatever he did he would have done with that sword-like singleness of heart. As it was, born of the times and of that fighting blood, he chose the greatest god he knew, and set forth into the universe to make men acknowledge his god to be the one true God, before whom all must bow. It was a magnificent imperialism of the spirit, incredible and not to be understood except by those who have been reared in it and have grown beyond it. Most of all are those yet in it unaware of what they are.

But to Andrew spiritual imperialism was as natural as the divine right of kings was to Charles the Second. Andrew, too, had that same naïve and childlike guilelessness of the king. He would have been pained and astonished if anyone had ever told him he was arrogant and domineering. Indeed, he did not seem so, his bearing was of such gentleness and dignity, his step quiet, his voice soft, his manner always restrained and controlled except for those rare strange sudden furies, when something he kept curbed deep in him broke for a moment its leash. Everyone was afraid of him at those moments. His children were terrified when they saw that quick working of his face, the sharp upthrust of his hand. Someone would be hurt—struck—his hand or his cane flying out. It was over in a second, and it broke through less and less often as he grew older, until at last it died altogether, I think, or distilled itself into a diffused strength and no longer burst forth in anger, so that in his last years he was mellowed to his heart's core.

But in his youth there were those swift furies in him. I know now he never allowed one to escape him without shame and contrition. I do not doubt that when he let his hand drop so suddenly and left the room so quickly he was going into his study to fall upon his knees and beg God's forgiveness. But I think it never occurred to him to beg forgiveness of any man. It really did not occur to him, for he was not humanly proud. If he had seen it as his duty to ask forgiveness he would have done it eagerly. He never shirked his duty. But it seemed important to him only to have God's forgiveness, to make sure that clear deep channel between him and God was not defiled. At all costs he kept it clear and deep, and so he lived happily. For he had this happiness: he espoused early a cause in which he believed all his life without a shadow of doubt. Not even his own mind betrayed him. He had his mind in inexorable control. He died, sure that he had chosen rightly, had believed wisely, and had achieved success in what he had done. There are not many to whom such happiness is given.

Being always perfectly happy he had a charm about him. He was quietly gay very often, sometimes full of jokes. I have often seen him sitting at table or in the stillness of evening after the day's work was over, when suddenly his blue eyes would brim with secret laughter and he would laugh silently. "What is it?" I always asked. Sometimes, rarely, he would tell me. But most often he would say simply, "I was thinking of something." I think he felt open laughter unbecoming. Yet sometimes when he did tell its cause he would choke and stammer with laughter. It always took us a little aback when he told us, because the thing he laughed at was often rather surprisingly simple, an incongruity of some sort. Carie smiled at him as she did at one of the younger children. This perception of the simple incongruous was as far as his humor went.

But it could be difficult at times, because if he disliked a person he did not conceal his laughter. For instance, he disliked women at best, but he especially and openly hated the large, florid, overconfident type which our Western civilization seems to have developed in such numbers. Once when he was quite an old man he sat at my table opposite a guest who was such a person. Andrew, disliking her at once, had sat in doughty silence, refusing to acknowledge her presence beyond a scant bow. She, rattling along in her voluble way, spoke of the ball she was going to attend after dinner at the American Consulate and worried as to whether or not she would "mind" dancing with the Chinese men who would be present. She had never danced with men of another race than her own. Andrew lifted his eyes from his plate alertly. I knew he hated the way she looked, her fat arms bare to the shoulder, her large bosom bursting under her tight gown. Bulk of flesh filled him with distaste to the point of rage. Now I saw his absent eyes take on their familiar mirthful, mischievous gleam. He began suddenly in that deceptive, slow, soft voice, "I should think a Chinese man could scarcely be found who—" I pressed his foot under the table, hard and quickly. The large lady's eyes glittered.

"Do have some—some coffee," I pleaded with her. "Oh, your dress is lovely," I babbled on. "That color is so becoming—just like your eyes!"

She turned toward me, flattered and effulgent. "Do you think so?"

"Yes, indeed—indeed," I cried. I kept my foot hard on Andrew's. He was stirring his cup of tea, shaking with silent laughter, forgetting everything except the picture he saw in imagination of this immense American supporting against her hugeness a slight Chinese figure in the foolishness of dancing. Afterwards when I remonstrated with him, as I dared to do in those days, he remarked calmly, "Well, the woman ought to be laughed at—she's a fool." Andrew was always very sure of himself.

"It was very unfortunate," Andrew used to say to us, "that your mother was given to seasickness. I remember she was seasick at once upon leaving the shores of America. I urged her to exert herself to control it, but she seemed determined to let it take its course. Control would have been possible in another less stubborn nature. But in her case she allowed seasickness to become aggravated so that she never really recovered."

"You don't mean she really could have helped it!" we cried, springing to Carie's defense.

"One has to make an effort," he remarked serenely. "Besides, it was most inconvenient."

So I do not imagine on that wedding journey across a stormy typhoon-ridden ocean that Andrew was a very good nurse to a seasick bride. He would of course have been very considerate in his inquiries, but he would not have known what to do for her. He was never ill himself. He ate, he told me with unconsciously pleasurable memory, his first raw oysters that night out of Golden Gate.

It was so rough that the first one slid down his throat before he swallowed it, so he could not get its taste. The second one he bit firmly. "With a little pepper and catsup," he remarked gently, "I found them eatable. I believe I ate twelve, but regretted afterwards that I had not stopped at six."

"You weren't seasick?" we inquired with malice.

"Not at all," he replied. "I have never been ill on the sea. I had merely a sense of regret for a few hours, but I kept my mind on other things."

He had a constitution of steel and a digestion which nothing could disturb. It was as near as he ever came to seasickness, and he could never understand the tortures of Carie's more delicately balanced body.

But Andrew was never ill in any way. For years on his journeys he ate what there was to be eaten. Hard-boiled eggs were a delicacy that Chinese farm wives set before him and he ate them. One night at home he saw hard-boiled eggs on a salad Carie had made.

"Twelve," he murmured gently. "I have eaten twelve hard-boiled eggs today."

"Andrew!" cried Carie, alarmed. "Why did you do it?"

"For Christ's sake," he said. "If I hurt the people's feelings they would not listen, and being poor, it was their best."

Once, to make conversation in a peasant home, he looked out over a field of whitely blooming buckwheat, and remarked that he liked buckwheat made into cakes. The housewife immediately hustled about and he found himself confronted with a huge plateful of thick, dry, enormous buckwheat cakes, with nothing on them. He plodded through as many of them as he could. Not then, nor any time he went to that house, did he ever shirk eating them, though he dreaded them and was dejected every time he felt it his duty to go there.

So when Carie was seasick he could not believe that if she tried she would not be better.

"An effort—" he would murmur above her distracted head.

"Oh, go away, Andrew!" she implored him. "Isn't there some book you ought to be studying?"

"Andrew has no conception—" she used to say to us over and over, under her breath. But in the next breath she begged, "You children mustn't pay attention to me. Your father's a wonderful man."

He was wonderful. He preached his first sermon in Chinese six months after his arrival. It is considered a fair feat if it is done after two years, so Andrew was a missionary prodigy. He was quite proud of himself, too, and told it many times with naïve pride, although it is only fair to say that he would always add with that subdued gleam in his blue eyes, "Of course it is another question as to whether anyone understood me or not. I never heard of any conversions as a direct result of it."

His own memories of their first landing upon Chinese shores were very unlike Carie's. She could not escape the misery of the people she saw about her. But Andrew was astonished at the comfort in which the missionaries lived.

"As soon as we landed," he said, "we were met by a delegation of older missionaries who were very glad to see me, since no new reinforcements had come for some years. We were taken to dine at Dr. Young Allen's home. The dinner was an excellent one—much too excellent for a missionary's table, I remember thinking at the time. But afterwards I heard that Dr. Young Allen engaged himself also in mercantile pursuits. He fell into these ways during the period of the Civil War when the home church was not able to continue his salary—I believe it was stoves."

"You went to sleep during dinner and Carie was ashamed," we told him, having heard Carie tell the same story.

"I don't remember anything of that," he said mildly.

"I bought my first overcoat in Shanghai," he went on. "It was an extravagance, I thought, but I was told it was essential."

Carie in the midst of all her seasickness had grown four wisdom teeth on her honeymoon and her rather small lower jaw was so crowded that she was miserable. Andrew took her to a dentist, for the only dentists in China then were in Shanghai, and waited while she had them out with no anaesthetic—four great strong new teeth. Carie always had beautiful sound teeth. Once when she was sixty years old a dentist called his pupils to look and see how perfect teeth might be at her age. They gathered around her, solemn young Chinese dentists, while she obligingly opened her mouth as wide as she could. She laughed as she told it. "They stared until I felt my mouth was full of their eyes," she said. But there was a little pride in her voice—she knew she had a good body. And the wisdom teeth had deep strong roots.

Immediately after the teeth were pulled they went on the junk to go by canal to Hangchow—I had the story from Andrew, not Carie—and a hemorrhage set in before they sailed and he had to take her back to the dentist.

"It was very inconvenient," he said, "but we started again with a delay of a little under two hours. I was eager to get at my work."

IV

THE fascinating thing about Andrew and Carie was that from the two of them we always got entirely different stories about the same incident. They never saw the same things or felt the same way about anything, and it was as though they had not gone to the same place or seen the same people. Andrew remembered nothing of the canal journey except long conversations with the senior missionary and an immense amount of progress in the language, while Carie spent the hours on the tiny deck under a big umbrella against the sun, staring at the slowly passing banks, the fields of rice being harvested, the little villages. I know—for how often have I walked through Chinese fields in September!—that the warm windless air was resonant with the syncopated beat of flails threshing out the rice from the threshing floors of earth. I know the deep blue skies above the shorn gold fields and the flocks of white geese picking up the scattered grains of rice. It is still hot, and little children tumble in the path, naked and brown with the summer sun, to fall asleep curled in the shade at the root of a tree. For the very air is sweet and somnolent with that broken rhythmic beating of the flails.

But Andrew was alert to the mission compound.

"Everything was much better than I had dreamed," he told me once. "The houses were big and clean and the meals were excellent. I had expected to live in small mud huts. I was uncomfortable in the midst of such comforts —good food, servants, space. Your mother put up some sort of pinkish curtains in our room. I thought they were too fancy and said so."

"Did she take them down?" I asked.

"No," he said, "she always had her own notions. But I was there very little. I spent my time downstairs in the study. We began to study Chinese the morning after my arrival. We began at eight and studied until twelve, and again at one until five o'clock. Then we took a walk for exercise. There were no textbooks worth the name, so we began reading the New Testament. The teacher read a line and we repeated it after him as nearly as possible in the same tones. We did this every day except Sunday."

"Didn't you get tired?" we asked. Carie had often grown tired. There was a bed of chrysanthemums against the grey brick compound wall and she sat by the window so that when she could not longer endure the drone of the old teacher's voice she could look at the flaming heavy-headed flowers. She would not let herself look at them often—only when she was so tired she could not bear it. And then when they faded, mercifully there was a heavenly bamboo near the window, hung with heavy plumes of scarlet berries. And sometimes wild geese flew across the piece of sky that stretched above the compound.

"Tired!" exclaimed Andrew. "How could I be tired when I was doing the one thing I most wanted to do—fit myself for the Work?"

All his thoroughness inherited from his Teutonic ancestors went into that study. He dug and delved among the roots of the language. He learned the two hundred and fourteen radicals and the tones of the words, the aspirates and non-aspirates. He mastered its grammar and explored its idiom. He began the study of the Confucian classics so that from the first he would have a cultured vocabulary and mode of expression. It was characteristic of the tenacity of his mind and the singleness of his purpose that the philosophy of Confucius, so essentially that of Jesus Christ, never once appeared to him as of importance. "Confucius says some very nice things," he was wont to say calmly, "but he knew nothing of God and of course understood nothing of the wickedness of human nature and the necessity of salvation from sin through our Savior, the Lord Jesus Christ."

He was exceedingly scornful in after years of those missionary souls, more delicately balanced, who saw in the wisdom of Confucius a means of a sort of salvation, after all. "He's off the track," he would say of such a soul, with a genuine sorrowful pity.

But Andrew found cause for endless astonishment at

his fellow missionaries. The people about him were as he expected them to be—unsaved. But he had not expected to find missionaries quite so human as they were. "Most of them," he said, "though good, were not very bright men." "That fellow!" he exclaimed of another. "He was lazy. He didn't want to leave the comforts of his home. He'd go to a chapel on the street once or twice a week and then wonder why the Lord didn't give him converts."

"They were very quarrelsome men," he said, remembering those early holy men of the church. "I remember how exceedingly astonished I was, when I was first sent to Soochow, to find Dr. DuBose and Dr. Davis, the only two white men in the city, one living at the north and one at the south, and never meeting or speaking to each other. When I went to see Dr. Davis and spoke of Dr. DuBose, he said, 'Oh, how I hate that man!'" He paused, and added solemnly, "I was shocked." Then he went on. "When I was sent up the river to Chinkiang there was Dr. Woodbridge and Dr. Woods. They spent much time playing chess, and were alternately friends and enemies. When I first arrived it was during a period of enmity. They were not speaking. Each poured out upon me the story of the other's total unfitness for the Work. I felt it my duty to listen to each impartially and to endeavor to reconcile them."

He smiled a wry smile.

"Did you succeed?" we asked.

"I succeeded to this extent—they united in turning on me!" He gave his dry silent laugh.

What Andrew never knew, and what I did not know until I grew up and saw for myself, was that, with all his seeming tranquillity, he was a warrior with the best of them, a son of God continually going forth to battle, a fighting angel. One of my earliest memories in that square mission bungalow was of Monday afternoons devoted to what was called "station meeting," a gathering of the resident missionaries. On Sunday everyone had been religiously whetted by three church services—not only religiously whetted but physically exhausted and emotionally strained. Monday was the day after. I have sat, hundreds of Mondays, a small bewildered child, looking from one stubborn face to the other of my elders, listening to one stubborn voice and then another. What the quarrel was about I never in those days quite knew because it so continually changed. A great deal of it was about money—whether Mr. Wang, the evangelist at the West Gate chapel, should get ten dollars a month instead of eight, for instance. I hoped for ten because I rather liked round-faced merry little Mr. Wang who brought me packages of sweet rice cakes on New Year's Day. Hours went into the discussion of two dollars. But it seemed the two dollars would give Mr. Wang notions—he might want twelve some day—there would be luxuries, perhaps—mission money was sacred—a trust. Mr. Wang must have only eight dollars. Carie got up and went out, her face very red. I followed timidly.

"What's the matter, Mother?" I wanted to know.

"Nothing," she said, pressing her lips together. "Nothing—nothing at all!"

But I saw everything in her face. I went back, crushed, only to find Mr. Wang was quite forgotten now and they were arguing over repainting the church door or about an appropriation for tracts or over opening a new station. Andrew was always wanting to expand the Work, to open more stations, and the others did not want him to do it. Listening to them, my heart swelled with helpless tears. It seemed to me they were always against Andrew and Carie, those men and women with their leathery skins and hard mouths and bitter determined eyes. Andrew sat there, never looking at them, but always out of the window, across the valley to the hills, that brow of his white and serene, his voice quiet and final. Over and over again he was saying, "I feel it my duty to push further into the interior. I regret if it is against your will, but I must do my duty."

Thus Andrew did his share of quarreling, but in his own fashion. He never obeyed any rules at all, because they always seemed to conflict with what was his duty, and he always knew his duty. The others might vote and decide, for the Work was supposed to be carried on by a sort of democratic decision of all the missionaries, subject to their financial boards in America. But Andrew listened only to God. Lack of money never stopped him. If he had no money, and he never had it, he wrote to anybody he knew who had any, asking for it shamelessly. If he got it, and he often did, he was supposed by mission rule to report it and put it into the common budget. But though he would report it if he thought of it, he never gave it up and he used it as he liked—always to push on into the interior, to open up new little centers for his preaching. I have seen other lesser and more bureaucratic missionaries grow almost demented trying to control Andrew. They shouted bitter words at him, they threatened him with expulsion if he did not cease disobeying rules, over and over they called him a heretic, once even called him insane because he seemed to hear nothing they said. He was a rock in the midst of all the frothing—unmoved, unresentful, serene, but so determined, so stubborn in his own way, that I know there have been those who, seeing that high, obstinate, angelic tranquillity, have felt like going out and groaning and beating their heads against a wall in sheer excess of helpless rage. But Andrew did not know even that they were angry with him. Had he not told them God's will? He must obey God's will.

Well, God's will led him along the line of battle all his life. He waged continual war—battle and skirmish, but no retreat. One of his wars, which time and his own determination won him at last, was on the subject of an educated Chinese clergy. When he went to China he found the Chinese clergy for the most part very nearly illiterate. They had been coolies, servants, gatemen in mission compounds, humble men who were easily converted and who more easily stepped into the slight supremacy of standing in a pulpit and haranguing a passing crowd. Andrew was shocked to the soul. He was a scholar and a lover of learning, and he perceived the intellectual quality of the Chinese and how little Chinese of worth and standing could respect these ignorant men. It was, he felt, to bring the Church into contempt.

It seems absurd now, more than half a century later, to realize what a tremendous uproar Andrew made by such a belief. He was called a heretic, he was denounced for liberalism and modernism, for not believing in the power of the Holy Ghost, for trusting to men's brains rather than to God's power—all the hue and cry familiar through centuries to those who have dared to differ from orthodox religion. For, cried the orthodox—do they not always so cry?—God could do anything. He could make a gateman into a great preacher. Human knowledge was nothing but deception, "filthy rags," St. Paul had taught them to call all human righteousness.

Andrew, his head high above the surge, began to gather about him a little group of young intellectuals, five or six, whom he taught in a class in his own study. They were already learned in their own language. He taught them history, religious philosophy, Hebrew, Greek, homiletics—all the things he himself had been taught in seminary. He continued that class over years, its members changing. He never used an uneducated man in any of his churches. Fifty years after he began that war he saw a thriving theological seminary established and he closed his class. His world had caught up to him.

Then there was that question of religious denominations. One of the astounding imperialisms of the West has been the domination over the Chinese of Methodists, Presbyterians, Baptists, and what not, to the number of well over a hundred different types of the Protestant Christian religion alone. This has been, in China, more than a spiritual imperialism—it has been physical as well. There has been much talk of political spheres of influence, of Japan and Germany and England and France, dividing China into areas for trade and power. But the missionaries divided China, too. Certain provinces, certain areas, were allotted to certain denominations for propaganda and there was supposed to be no overstepping.

Andrew was, of course, a born overstepper, because he always did as he pleased. He went where he pleased to preach. If some irate Methodist missionary pointed out that in a certain town there was already a Methodist chapel and that therefore Andrew had no right there, he pshawed and preached on briskly. Accused, he said calmly, "The Methodists aren't accomplishing anything there. The man at their chapel is a stick. I can't let all the people in that town go without the Gospel." Yes, I know he was maddening.

For, illogically, he could be merciless on any who stepped into his preserves. A bogey of our childhood was a certain one-eyed Baptist missionary who, I know now, was a harmless good man, not more obstinate in his ways than others, but who throughout my childhood I felt was a spirit of darkness. I gathered that impression from Andrew because the man believed in and taught immersion as the one true baptism, while Andrew, being Presbyterian, only sprinkled the heads of his converts. But the one-eyed Baptist went about in Andrew's territory telling everybody sprinkling was wrong.

It was a nice situation, humorous only to the impartial observer. For the ignorant people, believing that if a little water was a good thing for the soul, more was better, too often followed the one-eyed man, to Andrew's intense fury. Moreover, it seemed there were certain passages in the New Testament which disconcertingly supported the one-eyed missionary's theory that Jesus walked people entirely under the water. The only thing that really helped Andrew was that a good many of the Chinese were disinclined to get themselves wet all over, especially in the winter, so that immersion was unpopular except in the hot season.

The war went on year after year, and it was the more difficult because Carie maintained a friendship with the pleasant wife of the Baptist. We sat silent through many a meal while Andrew with unwonted fluency said what he felt about other denominations, especially about the folly of immersion, and most especially about the lunacy of telling ignorant people they must be immersed. In his defense it must be said that it was of course extremely trying for him to labor to secure a good Presbyterian convert in one season only to discover upon the next visit that he had been immersed into a Baptist. It was like harboring a cuckoo in the nest. One taught and labored and suffered all the trouble of instilling the fundamentals of Christianity into a heathen and at least one should be able to put down a new member in the statistics. It was nothing short of religious thievery when the member was added to the Baptist glory.

After thirty years of strenuous warfare, the situation was settled one morning by the one-eyed missionary being found dead in his bed of heart failure. Andrew felt he was completely vindicated. He was at the breakfast table when the sad news was brought in by the compound gateman. He poured tinned cream into his coffee and put in a little extra sugar before he answered. He secretly loved sugar and was very stern with himself about it. But this morning he stirred it up. Then he looked around at us all and said in a voice of calm and righteous triumph,

"I knew the Lord would not allow that sort of thing to go on forever!"

Afterwards he was a complete and untiring advocate of denominational union. But that is the story of another war and he died before it was finished.

The truth is that the early missionaries were born warriors and very great men, for in those days religion was still a banner under which to fight. No weak or timid soul could sail the seas to foreign lands and defy danger and death unless he did carry his religion as a banner under which even death would be a glorious end. The early missionaries believed in their cause as men these days do not know how to believe in anything. Heaven was actual, a space filled with solid goods. Hell did burn, not only for the evil unbelieving, but far more horrible, for those who died in ignorance. To go forth, to cry out, to warn, to save others—these were frightful urgencies upon the soul already saved. There was a very madness of necessity, an agony of salvation. Those early missionaries were fighting in a desperate cause—to save those who were being born more quickly, dying more swiftly than they could possibly be saved. They laid vast plans, they drew up campaigns over hundreds of thousands of miles, they sped swiftly from soul to soul. They even estimated two minutes to a soul to tell them the way of salvation. "Believe on the Lord Jesus Christ—you believe? Saved, saved!"

It is not a thing to smile at, not even in these days of casual disbelief. It was a terrible thing, a crushing horror, not upon the blessed ignorant who died peacefully and went to hell all unknowing, but upon those frantic desperate men and women who felt upon themselves the responsibility of saving souls. None but the strong could have borne the burden—none but the strong, none but the blindly hopeful, could have eaten, could have slept, could have begotten children and lived out their days under such oppression.

But they were strong. I have not seen anywhere the like of Andrew and his generation. They were no mild stay-at-homes, no soft-living landsmen. If they had not gone as daring missionaries, they would have gone to gold fields or explored the poles or sailed on pirate ships. They would have ruled the natives of foreign lands in other ways of power if God had not caught their souls so young. They were proud and quarrelsome and brave and intolerant and passionate. There was not a meek man among them. They strode along the Chinese streets secure in their right to go about their business. No question ever assailed them, no doubt ever weakened them. They were right in all they did and they waged the wars of God, sure of victory.

Ah well, they are all gone now! There are no more left like them. Those who take their place in our modern times are shot through with doubt and distrust of themselves and their message. They talk of tolerance and mutual esteem, of liberalizing education and of friendly relations and all such gentle feeble things. They see good in all religions and they no longer wage any more wars and they serve their lives out for a small security. There is no taste in them. I can hear Andrew reading sternly from the Book of Revelation, "So then because thou art lukewarm, and neither cold nor hot, I will spue thee out of my mouth!" The giants are gone.

My memory of that circle of half a dozen soberly dressed people is grim. Now, of course, after years away from them, after knowing what people are like in ordinary places, I realize the impossibility to which their human souls were stretched. The real story of life in a mission station has never yet been told. When it is told it must be told, if it is to be told truthfully, with such vast understanding and tenderness and ruthlessness that perhaps it never can be done justly. The drama in it is terrifying. Imagine two, four, five, six—rarely more—white men and women, some married to each other, the others starved without the compensation of being consecrated to celibacy, imagine them thrown together, hit or miss, without regard to natural congeniality of any sort, in a town or city in the interior of China, living together for years on end, without relief, in the enforced intimacy of a mission compound, compelled to work together, and unable, from the narrowness of their mental and spiritual outlook, to find escape and release in the civilization around them. Within those compound walls is their whole real world. Their real companionships are with each other, or else they live utterly alone. They seldom become proficient enough in the language to enjoy Chinese society or literature, even if their prejudice did not forbid it. There they are, struggling to maintain standards of Christian brotherhood, struggling against their own natural antipathies and desires, wasting their spirits in an attempt to be reconciled to that which is irreconcilable among them.

And what incredible stories, what pathetic, human, inevitable stories! They are hushed, guarded against, kept secret, for the sake of the Work, for the sake of the "home church," for shame's sake, for God's sake—but what stories!

There was that old white-haired gentle man who worked for so many faithful years, only to go at last so strangely mad, so quietly mad, shielded by his agonized loyal wife. The story crept out, as it always comes out, through servants. He had a concubine—a fresh-faced Chinese country girl. Yes, his wife knew. Yes, they had prayed over it in such distress, so long—there was that insatiable thirst in him for—for such things. It was hard to understand—he was so good, really. And then his wife had thought of old Abraham, longing for the young

Hagar, and it seemed to her she was like Sarah, and Sarah gave Hagar to Abraham. And God was not angry—God understood. But the story came creeping out, and the old white-haired pair were hastily retired.

And there was the strange little grey-eyed, brown-haired, pallid Chinese child, running about with a native pastor's flock of children. And there was the tall lonely missionary whose wife was years away, educating her own children at home. No one ever knew how that story came creeping out of a little village. An enemy did it, perhaps. No one is without enemies in China. But when the Chinese pastor was asked why among his dark brood there should be the one pale child with foreign eyes, he answered candidly enough, "The white man who is my head lives a very lonely life. And did not David take another man's wife, yet he was the Lord's beloved?"

And there were the two old missionaries, man and wife for forty years, living dangerous, brave, sacrificing lives, and suddenly their life fell into pieces when they were old, and the man, sensitive and worn to his bones, cried out that he had hated his wife for years, that his flesh had revolted at hers, and he had lived in desperate unhappiness. He cried over and over only one thing, shuddering, "I don't want ever to hear her voice again. I don't want to feel the touch of her hand!"

And there is the story of that pleasant-looking missionary, subject for years to moods of mania, when he imagined his kind dark-eyed wife was unfaithful to him, and he would seize a knife from the table or a chair or anything at hand, and try to kill her. Their four little children grew up with the horrible secret and not one of them spoke, because their mother, after the mood was over and after he had made her do penance by crawling around him on her hands and knees, laid it upon them with passion that they were never to tell. So they never told. They grew up with a strange quiet tensity of look, but no one knew. Then the faithful wife died and the missionary married again, a gentle spinster, and she would not tell, and so it went until at last he revealed the truth himself in a fit, and all the years of torture came to life again in the shuddering words of the children, released at last to speak.

And no one has told the story of the spinsters for Christ's sake, the women who in the sweet idealism of their youth go out to lonely mission stations. Year by year they grow paler and more silent, more withered and more wistful, growing sometimes severe and cruel with their fellowmen, and sometimes, too, growing into miracles of pure and gentle selflessness. Most of them never marry, because no man ever asks them—there is none to ask them. Sometimes they marry a man inferior, an older widower, a rough river captain—even, sometimes, though this is never to be told, their Chinese associates. But that is so rare I think it truly need not be told.

And those missionary widowers, marrying so quickly when their wives die that even the polygamous Chinese wonder! The missionary cemeteries are full of wives. I think of one black shaft of a tombstone in a certain walled spot beside the Yangtse River where an old son of God lies buried with three wives and seven of his children about him. But the shaft is raised only to him. Yes, the blood of such white men runs hotter than the blood of the heathen, even though they are men of God.

Yet to understand the impossible narrowness of that mission life is to forgive every bond that is sometimes burst. In that hot foreign climate, in the storms of wind and dust, in the floods and wars and risings of mobs against them, in such uneasiness of life, in such impossibility of achieving what they have set themselves, in bitter isolation from their kind, in the inward oppression of their own souls, that oppression which looks out of their somber eyes and sounds in their voices, apathetic if they are not angry, the wonder is not that men of God quarrel with each other so often, but that they do not kill each other or themselves more often than they do.

They do sometimes kill themselves. There was that missionary wife who rose from her husband's bed after she had borne him eight children and ran in her white gown through the night on a Chinese street and leaped from a cliff into the Yangtse River. And there was that gay and pretty Southern girl who rose in another night and crept downstairs into her own kitchen and with a common chopping knife tried to cut her throat and could not die, and she went up into the attic, her husband and her four little children sleeping, and found a rope and hung herself, and she leaped from the window and the rope broke and still she could not die, and she staggered, dripping blood, upstairs again into the bathroom and found poison and so died at last. There are such stories, but nobody wants them told, for the Work must go on. I say the wonder is not that there are these stories and scores like them, but that there are not many more than there are. Conversion does not really change the needy human heart.

But of course I only came to know all this afterwards. In those days of my childhood I may as well confess I was afraid of Andrew and all of them. My own private real life was lived entirely elsewhere in a place where there was no God at all.

There were mornings, bright sunny spring mornings, when one woke up to imagination. Usually it was a day when Andrew was going away on a journey. I may as well tell still more of the truth. A certain relief came over us all when he was going away on one of his preaching tours. The servants ran briskly to fetch and pack. There was always a bedding roll to get ready, a long bag of brown homespun cotton cloth into which was put a thin mattress, a blanket, and a pillow. Andrew was fastidious about lice in inn beds. If he were traveling by land this bedding was thrown across the back of his white donkey. Then he, wearing a sun helmet and a light grey cotton suit, or earlier his Chinese robes, and carrying a cane under his arm to beat off dogs, would straddle the donkey and the bedding roll, his long legs dangling until his feet were not two inches from the ground. He always said drily that if the donkey tried to kick up he simply held his feet on the ground. But it was a sturdy beast and trotted off with dogged gayety, its ears cocked wickedly, tail swishing. We watched that gaunt indomitable figure disappear down the cobbled, willow-shaded lane, and then a sense of peace fell over us all. The servants dawdled. Carie went to the organ and sang a long time or she read a book, and I—I went out into the garden and played all day there was no God. And Carie often helped unconsciously by saying at twilight, "We'll skip prayers tonight and take a walk instead—just for once God won't mind." God! There hadn't been any God all day.

On one such evening I carried imagination to a dangerous pitch. I decided not to say my prayers at all. I could not sleep for a long time, dreading the darkness. For in the darkness I knew of course there really was a God—there was that Eye that saw everything. But I stuck to my wickedness and fell asleep to wake, to my astonishment, perfectly safe, the peaceful summer sunshine streaming in my window. I never feared Andrew quite so much again. God had not done anything to me.

Now that I am no longer young, I know that Andrew never meant to frighten a little child or dreamed that he did. There were times, I remember now, when he came back from his long tours spent and weary but in a sort of glory of content, his work well done, God well served. He seldom saw beauty, and yet there were times when he said at supper, "The mountains were pretty today, covered with red and yellow azaleas everywhere." Sometimes he even brought back an armful of the flowers, if it so happened that his heart was content with what had happened to him. Sometimes he told us what he had seen —a small hill panther had crouched at the side of the road, and he had not known whether to go on or turn back, but he had promised to be at a certain village at noon and there would be those who waited for him. So he went on without seeming to notice, and the beast had not sprung. Wolves he saw often in winter, sometimes running down into the fields where the farmers chased them. But I was disappointed when I first saw a wolf because it looked like a big village dog and little more, except it was an odd dull grey in color.

In the spring Andrew was always gone. He grew restless as winter closed and as soon as the spring floods began to well into the canals from the river, swollen with melting snows in the upper gorges, he began to plan his long preaching tours by junk or upon his white ass. When Carie lay dying she said to me, knowing well enough that some woman would have to look after Andrew, "Look out for spring! About the first of April he gets hard to manage. It won't matter if he's eighty, he'll want to get away over the country and behind the hills preaching." Well, it was a good thing he always had the Gospel to preach so that he could go into all the world and be happy, feeling it was his duty. Not everyone is so lucky. But then I always said Andrew had a happy life. God always seemed to have told him to do what he would have wanted to do anyway.

In all my life I heard Andrew speak of only two men with unmeasured praise, and though I never saw them myself, for I was born too late for that, I have always thought of them as giants. For all I know they may have been men of ordinary size, but I see them tall like gods. They take their place with Goliath and David, and for goodness they stand among the elder prophets. Otherwise Andrew would not have praised them. For he might give away silver and gold carelessly, but he never so gave his praise. I waited years to hear a word of approbation from his lips, and when it came I knew I deserved it or he would not have given it to me then.

It seemed that Andrew was utterly dissatisfied with the plans of expansion in the narrow mission group in which he worked. "Creeping from village to village!" he exclaimed. "Satisfied with a street chapel or two in a town! Why, we have to think in terms of a continent and of millions of people!" He began to plan a scheme of rapid northward expansion which seemed nothing short of insanity to his fellow missionaries. But opposition was energy to Andrew.

It happened that this was the time when Carie came down with tuberculosis and they went to a northern seacoast where she could recover. While she was busy about this, Andrew investigated, as he set forth on his preaching tours, the methods of missionaries in that province of Shantung, a region which belonged to another religious denomination. So he found the two giants, whose names were Corbett and Nevius. They did not work together. In fact, I believe they were mortal enemies. But both were so statesmanlike, both so large in their plans, that Andrew admired them completely. He went with them, listening, observing, learning. For years he discussed the relative merits of their opposing systems of spreading the Gospel. One worked extensively, over wide areas, taking advantage of every chance, content with less than satisfactory results sometimes in order to see constant expansion. The other worked intensively, perfecting and completing each center before he opened another, making a continuous chain of churches rather than scattering them widely. Both were men of shining intellect, imperious wills, and volcanic physical energy. But one was a rough crude son of an American farmer and the other a polished and cultivated gentleman. Out of such extremes do sons of God come.

Andrew, in the illimitable extravagance of his ambition, planned to adopt the best in both their methods. He would expand and develop, too. "Those months were the most useful of my life," he wrote. "Those two great missionaries set the plan of my own missionary career." When Carie was well again and they returned to Central China, he was in a frenzy to begin his real work. He had already been nearly five years in China, but he felt that only now had he really begun. He left his family in a rented house in Chinkiang and set sail eagerly up the Grand Canal, alone.

V

I KEEP forgetting, as I tell this story, to say anything about the birth of Andrew's children. I am possessed by Andrew. I see him, as I so often saw him, eagerly, eternally setting out on a new journey. I hear him in his old age telling me, in his fragmentary fashion, his own story, and he never said anything about the children. I was not born yet, so I cannot tell my own story of him then. But when he sailed up the Grand Canal to begin his work of opening up new territories he had a son living and a daughter dead and another child soon to be born. Carie told me that.

He never told me anything of the birth and death of his children. He did tell me, chuckling, that in a city up the canal where he decided to make his first center, he rented what he called "a splendid house" for almost nothing at all. No Chinese would live in it because it was haunted by a fox. "It was nothing but a weasel," he said with a dry laugh, seeing no likeness between their fears and his own secret twinges at ghost stories. He had the place whitewashed and made clean and then went and fetched his family and left Carie to settle things while he traveled northward. But he always spoke a little fondly of that house. He was rather proud of himself for having found it, and he thought of its simple comfort warmly when he was on his prodigious journeys. I have no picture of it from him for he could not tell such things. But they bought one of the stoves from Shanghai and it was warm in winter and he had a study of his own where he could put his books, and he had a good student lamp on a big Chinese table and an easy chair. Those were things to remember when he lay on a brick bed in an inn or jogged over the intolerably rough roads on his donkey.

That he might travel more quickly he planned and made with a Chinese carpenter's help a sort of wagon with springs of a crude kind. He stood by the ironsmith's forge while they were being beaten out upon the anvil, and around him gathered a great crowd, staring at his strangeness, dubious of those great iron pieces. Were they not parts of some sort of foreign sword? Then he bought a mule and hitched it to the wagon and clattered up and down the countryside in great content, to the excitement of all beholders.

So great was the envy of his wagon, however, that at last some robbers heard of it and came and took it and all he had, except his tracts and Bibles which they threw into a ditch. And Andrew walked thirty miles barefoot and in his underwear, and upon his back were three great open cuts which they had given him when he resisted. For he had put up a stout fight, Carie discovered upon close questioning. She got the story out of him by bits. Yes, of course he had said he wouldn't give up his cart. Why should he? What did he do? Why, he hit them with his whip until they pushed him off the seat, and then he jumped up and cracked a lot of their heads together! He was so much taller that he could do it, but there had been too many of them—he could not crack enough of them quickly enough. Carie washed his wounds and bound them and he complained bitterly of having to sleep on his stomach for weeks, and more out of his irritation than anything else he went to the local magistrate and demanded his cart and mule again. The magistrate was a peace-loving, opium-smoking old scholar and he said mournfully it was impossible—he would give Andrew money. But Andrew insisted on the cart and the mule. He threatened international complications if they were not forthcoming. Andrew always made use of international treaties and extraterritoriality. Had he not a perfect right to preach the Gospel? The magistrate sighed and promised. The mule never came back—the magistrate apologized profusely and said unfortunately he had been eaten. But the cart came back quite ruined, and Andrew looked at it a little grimly but satisfied. At least no one else was getting the good out of it. He went back to donkey riding again, as being safer and more suitable after all to a man of God.

This was Andrew's method of procedure in his days of militant expansion. He would ride into a large village or into a town he had chosen as his next center and search out the largest tea shop and tether his donkey to one of the bamboo poles that held up its blue cotton awning and go in and sit down at a table near the street. His great height, his big nose, his bright blue eyes, his whole most foreign-looking figure would within a quarter of an hour draw a great crowd. Within an hour, or as long as it took for the telegraphic speed of the mouth-to-mouth message, "A foreign devil is in the tea house on the Big Bridge," everybody in the town would be there, unless they were bedridden. The tea shop keeper never knew whether to be pleased or terrified at such a mob. Certainly he never had such a customer before as this giant.

But Andrew smiled amiably and drank bowls of tea, and asked questions about the town—how many families lived here, and what was the chief business, and who was the magistrate? The few of the more bold among the crowd pressing against him answered, a little fearfully—for why should a foreign devil want to know these things about them?

Then the boldest would ask a question of him: "What honored country is yours, Foreign Devil?"

"My unworthy country? America!"

The crowd breathed more freely. Ah, America—America was good. There was an unblinking pause while they stared at him. So this was how Americans looked! They examined him minutely, and made the next question. "What is your business, Foreign Sir?"

"I am a Jesus church man."

Again the crowd stared, nodding to each other. Jesus church—they had heard that word. Well, it was a good thing—all religions were good—all gods were good. They felt easier, having placed him.

But Andrew shook his head. Not all gods were good, he said firmly. There were false gods—gods of clay and stone—but his was the one true god. They listened, humoring him. After all, he was a foreigner—he could scarcely be expected to know manners.

He handed out tracts and now they shook their heads. "None of us can read," they said apologetically. It was better to take nothing from him, not strange papers with pictures. "I have some books, too," he said. "I sell them for a penny apiece." Well, selling was different. That was to be understood. A few in curiosity, two or three, fumbled in their belts for pennies and took the small paper-bound books. He sat there for an hour or two, and then he went away. Behind him the crowd made their judgment—a harmless good man doing a religious penance, doubtless. He must have made a vow to a god to do a good deed, else why leave home to wander over the earth? He was laying up merit for himself in heaven, it must be. Perhaps he had committed a crime in his own land. Well, he was an ugly fellow with such big hands and feet and a nose like a plough, and eyes like a demon's—but a good man, doubtless, selling his little books to buy his rice on his journey. Well, it was time to go home.

In a few days Andrew would be back. There would be a crowd again, not so large, but friendly and familiar. "Back again, Foreigner! You like our village!"

"Yes, it is a good village. I should like to preach here."

"Preach—preach what you will—we will listen!" they said, laughing.

So Andrew stood up in the tea shop to preach. "For God so loved the world, that he gave his only begotten Son, that whosoever believeth in him should not perish, but have everlasting life." Out of these words, solemnly repeated, Andrew had worked a brief compact exposition of the whole scheme of salvation. God—His son—believe—not perish—everlasting life. His whole creed was there. "I devised a short sermon," he wrote gravely, in after years, "which comprehended all the essentials of Salvation, so that the unsaved soul, hearing perhaps but once, could understand and so take upon itself its own responsibility."

Again and again Andrew would return to that place until his figure became familiar to them, and then he would look about for a room to rent, a room that opened upon the street. When it was found it was whitewashed clean, some cheap wooden benches bought, a rough table for a pulpit, a text painted on the wall behind it. Behind the table Andrew stood regularly to preach, twice a week, three times perhaps, as often as he could, and the crowd came and went. Weary farmers set down their baskets on their way back from market and listened as they rested. Curious citizens came in and sat a while to hear a new thing. Mothers came in out of the sun to sit on the benches and nurse their babies.

But the women were always an aggravation to Andrew. "They never really listen," he complained. "They call across the room to each other, asking silly questions about cooking and children. They never understand anything, so it is no use wasting time on them."

"Well, I suppose they have souls, Andrew," Carie always said with spirit.

But Andrew would never answer. It was evident that he doubted it. Anyway, a woman's soul could scarcely count as a full soul. In his records of converts he always noted them. "Seventy-three received this year (fifteen women)." A really successful year was when the percentage of women was low. When they came up for examination into church membership he never treated them quite as he did the men. "They haven't much real idea of what they are doing," he said. "It's beyond them."

As soon as there was a little group—two, three, four converts—he pushed on to fresh villages, leaving in his place an older convert from an earlier center, whom he had trained to be a preacher of sorts. Twice a year, on his long spring and autumn tours, he would visit every village, examine new converts, baptize those who seemed to him sincere, hear complaints and troubles, and sprinkle the heads of infants whose parents were converts. One of the proofs which he insisted showed the stupidity of women was that these mothers whose babies were sprinkled could never understand that it did not make the infants members of the church. Time and again at a communion service I have seen his face grow stiff with horror as he saw an innocent Chinese mother cram the holy bread into a tiny baby's mouth and pour in a gulp of wine. There was always a roar of protest from the baby—not one of them seemed willingly a Christian! Andrew always "spoke" to the mothers. They looked at him, frightened at his serious, shocked face.

"Will he die of it?" one sometimes whispered.

"No—no—it isn't that," he would explain. "Don't you see . . ." he went on to explain. They listened, trying to understand. They all listened, men and women, as he preached, trying to understand.

There was something about those little handfuls of converts that wrings my heart even at the distance of these years. They were infinitely pathetic somehow. Why had they come out from among their people to listen to this stranger? Why did they come out from the safety of their people to believe him? They were so alike in every village

—one looked and saw the same ones, the old woman whose patient face was shaped and sculptured by disappointment, deep and long. Life was nearly over, and then what was there? Her eyes were always too intelligent, too profound. She had been born with more wisdom than her fellows. It had not been quite enough for her, the common life of marriage and bearing children. She had enough for all this and something more. Ask her why she was there and she would answer a little painfully, "I have tried all the other ways to find peace, but I have not found peace."

"What ways, lady?"

"I have prayed to many gods. I have listened to many priests, but I have this aching in me." She puts an exquisite old hand delicately upon her breast.

"What is it that aches there?"

"I do not know."

"You have sons?"

"Yes, I have sons—three sons—it is not that."

"You have everything?"

"Everything—but no peace."

"How do you know you have no peace?"

"I wonder so much—night and day I am restless with wonder."

"What wonder?"

"I ask myself, why am I alive? Why are all these about me alive? What does birth matter and marriage and birth again, since at last there is only death? What does this mean?"

"And you hope to find peace here?"

"I do not know—only here is a god I have not known, and here is a strange priest I have not heard."

"You believe what he says?"

"I do not know, but I feel at least he is to be believed because he so believes himself. It is something when a priest believes himself. So I will try."

There is another old woman who sits near her, a common old soul with a pocked face who sits sleeping while Andrew preaches, her jaw hanging.

"Good mother, why are you here?"

She grunts, opens her eyes and laughs and rubs her head to wake herself.

"Why, you see, it is like this. I have no son, accursed that I am, and only two daughters, now married. I am old, so my man, who is only a clod at best, has not fed me for these ten years, and I do a little work as I can. I mend socks for the soldiers or I wash vegetables for an innkeeper or I scrub out night pots for the slaves of the rich who are too dainty to do such things for their mistresses—anything I can I do, because I cannot be always going to my daughters' doors with my bowl empty, or their husbands make it hard for them. So I must shift for myself. I came here to see if this foreigner would give me a little work."

"But you said you believed in his talk! You let him put water on your head!"

"Eh, yes—a little water—well, I let him have his way, because I thought he would be pleased and help me a little. Do you know him? Will you speak for me? Tell him . . ."

On the other side of the aisle where the men sit, there is that slight pale lad who sits with his knees crossed and one restless foot tapping the brick floor as he listens and does not listen to Andrew. For sometimes he opens a hymn book restlessly and sometimes he stares out of the little dirty-paned window.

"Why have you come, young sir?"

"I want to learn English."

"Why?"

"I want to get away from this miserable village. I want to get a job in a big city—Shanghai. If I could speak English I could get a job in a big foreign office."

"Who told you?"

"I have heard it said."

"You do not believe what he says?"

"This tall foreigner? I do not believe in any religion. I do not want religion. I want money. I want to see the world."

There is an old man—there is always an old man.

"Old sir, why have you taken the bread and wine?"

"Religion is good—all religion is good—it brings peace."

"Do you believe in other gods as well as this man's god?"

He smiles gayly and delightfully, his face as calm as a Buddha's. "I believe in all gods—all gods are good."

There is a tall Mohammedan. There is Arab in him; it is in the lean line of his cheek and in the curve of his nostril and in the thin arch of his lips.

"You have left Allah?"

"I see that Allah for whom I have sought is this man's God. He has compelled me to belief."

"How has he compelled you?"

"There is fire in him. There is fire in me. The flame in his soul leaned over and caught at the flame in me, and I was compelled."

"Have you not been disowned by your friends, your family?"

"Yes, I am disowned. I have no friends, no family. My name is gone from the family names. They struck it away on the day when I told them I was a Christian."

"What will you do now?"

"I follow after this man."

"And then?"

"I will follow him."

This man indeed followed Andrew all his life, and Andrew made him into a great preacher. He might have been Andrew's brother, they were so alike; both of them tall and lean, their faces spare, their noses bold. Andrew was fair, and the wind and sun had burned his face dark red, and the same wind and sun had burned the Mohammedan's face a dark copper brown. But they were soul brothers.

Thus they came, some for one thing, some for another. Those who came only to see and hear a new thing fell away. But there was always the handful who stayed to listen, to learn, to eat at last the bread and drink the wine. Then, having eaten and drunk, they clung to Andrew. For after that they were lost. They had separated themselves from their fellows and they could never be again as they had been. Christians! The color of their souls was changed. They had taken foreign substance into themselves. They could never go back to the old close, quarreling, merry-making life of streets and tea shops and market-places. Nor could they ever again go before the old gods. Their brothers, their fellows, never trusted them wholly again. They had eaten the flesh and drunk the blood of a new god.

Somewhere in this time Comfort was born, but it was entirely insignificant because it made no difference to Andrew, especially since she was a girl. Yet he should have been a little grateful because she helped him, merely by being born. It happened this way. Carie had lost two children in swift succession, and suddenly she broke, she whom Andrew had always thought was so headstrong, so invincible. She broke and begged to be taken home.

Nor was Andrew himself unmoved. Carie told me once she had never seen tears in Andrew's eyes, but the nearest she had seen to a dimness in their clear bright blue was when his son Arthur died. That night when his little fair body lay waiting for burial, Andrew and Carie read together their usual scripture before they went to bed. Andrew turned to the story of King David mourning over his dying son. "O my son Absalom, my son, my son Absalom!"

"He choked a little," Carie said. "Then he went on and read the rest in his usual firm way. 'Would God I had died for thee, O Absalom, my son, my son!' He shut the Bible and was himself again."

For Andrew so believed in God and in Divine Providence that it was not in him to grieve. "The Lord giveth and the Lord taketh away. Blessed be the name of the Lord!" For him this vast serenity covered the universe.

But when the second child, a girl, died, Carie became nearly demented with grief. Years after he said in a shocked voice, "I never saw so hard a heart, so unreasoning a mind, as were hers in those days. Nothing I could say would move her. The doctor in Shanghai said she must be diverted or she would lose her reason. So I engaged passage for Europe. I would have preferred the Holy Land, but she would not go there because somebody had told her the village dogs were mangy like those in China and the people were poor. So we went ashore at Brindisi. I remember at Lucerne there was very nice honey for breakfast. In Rome there was a great number of naked statues. It seemed strange when one considers that Rome is the center of the Christian religion. For I suppose, though Popish, Catholicism is nevertheless a form of Christianity. I grew tired of Europe."

The truth was, of course, that Andrew grew quickly tired of anything except his work. For he had made huge plans for which any life was too short. The continent of China lay before him. Only by unceasing steady marching on could he succeed in completing, before he died, the campaign he had so plainly in his mind. Carie used to say she believed Andrew's brain was a map of China. He knew every province, every city, every river and town. He marked as his own those where he had planted his little chapels. Once one was established, and added to his chain of centers, he went on to new territory.

To this unending zealous preaching, this desperate salvation, he brought a deep inward emotional tensity that ate him up, body and soul. It flamed in him like fever under his serene exterior. When he was visiting cathedrals in Rome and Florence, he was still really in China, planning, planning, thinking, worrying lest the apostle Chang was too weak to be left alone, lest Li would be too domineering over the souls left in his charge.

But he was more afraid of his fellow missionaries than of anyone, lest they change his plans, dismiss or move his ministers, disturb with meddling his intricate campaign. When he came back to the hotel room he would take a sheet of paper and begin printing in square, clear Chinese letters his warnings and admonitions and instructions. "Do not listen," he wrote over and over to his comrade, Ma, once the Mohammedan, now Ma the Christian, "do not listen to any of the others, but to me who am your spiritual brother. Remember the plan we made together—follow it until I come." He stared out into the Roman street and saw the sunlight fall upon a marble church. "Rome is full of images," he said, "infinitely worse in their nakedness than the gods of the heathen." He would put his hand to his forehead in a gesture of agitation. "I ought to be about my father's business," he muttered. "I must be about my father's business!"

He went about Europe like a chained and quarrelsome lion, intolerant of all local customs. He was particularly furious at the incessant tipping. What—give a fellow he had never seen a sum of money large enough to hire a week's preaching of the Gospel, enough to buy an Old and New Testament, for carrying his bags? He lugged them himself, striding into hotel lobbies, brushing aside lackeys like flies. Only once was he beaten. He put Carie and Edwin into a train for France, and then, since there were ten minutes to wait, he went into the station to the lavatory. There he glared down the station attendant who held out his hand and strode on. But Andrew was worsted for once. The attendant locked him in and listened unmoved to Andrew's poundings and all but profanity. No one knows what Andrew said, since the attendant spoke no English and Andrew would say nothing himself beyond the bare facts. He came loping toward the train at the last minute, to the intense relief of Carie and Edwin. "Got locked in," he muttered, panting.

Carie instantly saw what had happened. "You have to pay them a little," she said.

"I wouldn't have if the train hadn't been going," Andrew said, firmly, finding his breath.

"After all, it's their country," Carie said gently. "We're foreigners here."

"That doesn't excuse robbery," said Andrew. Obviously there had been a tussle of wills, and as Andrew said, the train was going. The sole effect on him was to make him more obdurate than ever. He was particularly triumphant over the French and came more nearly than any other American ever did toward no tipping in France. Yet Andrew cared nothing for money—he could give it away with mad generosity when it was to buy Testaments and tracts and books of biblical research, or if it was to help a struggling divinity student toward graduation from seminary. But merely to give it—that was as foolish as it was to waste time away from the Work. He felt it equal sin, and he was always intolerant of sin. Years later his too sensitive children suffered and shrank from the contempt upon lackey faces as his tall lean figure marched by, laden with bags and bundles.

"People don't," they murmured in the misery of adolescence.

But Andrew set his big jaw firmly. People! He listened only to God.

After Europe, he looked with impatience toward his own country. There at last was a Christian nation, where men were honest and not looking always and only for money. He was droll with suppressed gayety on the day the ship docked at last at New York. He carried the bags ashore and deposited them abruptly in the nearest horse cab.

"Take me to a decent and reasonable hotel," he commanded the driver.

Carie, with the memory of the fray in Europe, said with unusual caution, "Hadn't you better ask the fare?"

But Andrew, with unusual recklessness, said, "We are in a Christian country now, thank God!"

They drove rattling through streets they did not know. "It's a long way," Carie said.

"Pshaw, Carie, the man knows what he is doing," Andrew replied. The horse stopped at a jerk of the bridle before a modest hotel.

"How much?" asked Andrew.

"Five dollars," the cabman said.

Andrew was dashed. Five dollars! It was a lot of money. But it had been a long drive. He paid, still in high humor. "We're home," he said, climbing the stairs with Carie and Edwin. They entered the room which they had taken. Carie walked directly to the window, as she always did in a strange place. She gasped.

"Why—why—Andrew, come here!" she cried, and burst into laughter.

"What is it?" he said in alarm. He came to her side and his gaze followed her pointing finger. There, not two blocks away, was the ship they had left nearly an hour before.

"What are you laughing for?" said Andrew, with a certain grimness. Five dollars!

"Because," she gasped,—"because it's such a—a Christian country!"

They went home by train, down through the states, through wooded hills that looked strange and furred after the shorn Chinese hills, over rivers that looked like creeks after the flooding Yangtse and the Yellow River, through towns whose houses looked unreal, they were so orderly and clean after the heaped mud and the confusion of Chinese villages. For ten years in China Andrew had not even seen a train, and he took an innocent pleasure in speed and ease, although still not too much ease. To have ridden in a Pullman he would have thought unbecoming in a missionary. What, take the money the church had gathered that the Gospel might be spread in heathen lands and spend it upon a softer bed for his body and for the bodies of his wife and children! He would have been made miserable. They traveled tourist or in day coaches, and even so he doubted the luxury. As for dining cars, he looked on them as sinful extravagance. To pay so much for mere food! He bought sandwiches and enjoyed them doubly as food and sacrifice.

The return home was a strange division. When ten years earlier he and Carie had gone away, they had felt they were leaving home indeed, forsaking father and mother to be worthy of their cause. The great old sprawling farmhouse had stood as certainly for home on this earth as heaven above was home for the soul. His parents had seemed endless in life, secure upon their land. But now he came back to find that the house, the home, was like a shell outgrown. His eyes had seen strange things. His feet had traveled many miles over other soil. He had begotten children under another roof and three of them lay buried in foreign earth. This old farmhouse was shrunken and old—and gone into decay. What had seemed so spacious and sound in his youth was grown into an old frame structure that needed paint and patching. The wooden pillars of the porches sagged, the roof leaked and the fence was so broken that the pigs could come in easily now. Within the house the hot old man still lived, but his heat had passed into smoldering. The quarrel between him and the woman had never mended. Every night he lay on the floor before the fire as he always had, staring into the coals, and she berated him in the same way for not sitting decently in the armchair opposite her own.

"Foolishness—you're getting old—you'll catch your death . . ."

It was true that of the two of them she was the stronger, the quicker, the neater. But then she did not fret herself as he did. She did nothing except sit on the porch or by the window and enjoy herself. Every now and again, upright and chipper, she would dart into the kitchen and find something to eat, a wedge of pie, a slice of salt-rising bread and apple butter, a cold fried chicken leg, a piece of ham, and with this she went back to enjoy herself.

"Snacking!" the old man would grunt. "Everlasting snacking!"

But she stayed as lean and strong as a hickory tree and lived far beyond him.

Every son had long gone out of the house except the youngest, and now he was grown and chafing to go. Son after son, they had gone out to preach and he wanted to go, because he too had the call. But the old man would not let him. One of the boys had to stay on the land. So the youngest son, tall and with the ice-blue eyes they all had, pushed the plough rebelliously and planned how as soon as the old man was dead he would be as good as his brothers. He would go to school and to seminary and stand in a pulpit and direct the people and tell them what was God's will. Meantime he married a buxom Irish girl with snapping black eyes, a famous cook and housekeeper. It was she who scrubbed and cleaned, baked and mended in the house, and added her word to the old man's or to the old woman's. She had a tongue of her own and an Irish temper, the kind the black-haired, black-eyed Irish have, and her cheeks were red, and her mouth sullen. Yet her heart was kind enough and her table was laden with food and anybody was welcome to sit down to it.

But the brothers and their wives were scattered over the states. David the learned had long been minister in the small village which had been Carie's home, Hiram the handsome had married a young beauty and blue-stocking and knew what a rare thing he had done. He was preaching in the South. Isaac was in Missouri, frail still from the years in prison, Christopher the Methodist was doing what the others grimly called "rampagin' around in the Methodist church." John the prudent, married to his rich widow, was managing her fortune, living in her huge comfortable brick house in the midst of broad and fertile acres and being elected for legislature. The house was empty of them all.

Andrew could not stay there, either. When he came home the old necessities fell upon him—cows to be milked, hay to be cut, horses to be fed. He fell into the old destroying labor and it was horrible to him. Every moment he was mindful that there were millions in China dying without the knowledge of God which he was able to give them to save their souls, and here he was milking cows and making hay! The old dreadful impatience came upon him.

And he was still Andrew the younger. The moment he came into this house he ceased to feel himself God's chosen. He became the younger son, less favored than any of the others. His mother, staring at him, remarked that he was yellow. His father snorted, "Heathen climate and eatin' heathen stuff!"

His hands grew hard and broken again at the nails. He had for years been secretly fastidious about his hands, ever since one of his brothers—Hiram, perhaps—had teased him about their size and boniness. "They look like an old man's hands," he always said. And his mother, hearing, always remarked placidly, "Andy ever did have hands like an old man, even when he was a baby." When he was really an old man his hands were extremely beautiful, large and skeleton thin, but delicate and full of grace. But then Andrew hated manual labor, although he did it conscientiously, as he did everything, to his best ability, hating it.

In after years the one great grievance he kept remembering of this first visit home was that no one asked him anything about his life or his work.

"I couldn't understand it," he said earnestly. His blue eyes were full of pain and clear wonder. "They never asked me anything about China."

It was an old hurt, carried in his heart over all the years. For he had come home a man, full in stature and wisdom, ripe with experience beyond any of theirs. He had been far beyond the horizon of hills and fields, beyond even the West that seemed so far, beyond the seas. He had eaten strange foods, had walked the streets of other countries and had learned to speak a foreign tongue. But here he was only Andrew come home again. No one cared that he spoke, read, and wrote Chinese excellently; no one asked him, "What do they eat over there and what do they wear?" They examined briefly a few gifts Carie brought. The old man was far more pleased when she took his old coat and ripped it apart and turned it and made it look new again.

Andrew, dwelling upon it when he was an old man, said, the painful dry red creeping into his cheeks, "They said I was very quiet and that I didn't talk. But they didn't ask me anything. Why should I tell them what they did not care to know?"

They were an undemonstrative clan. Carie said once, laughing, with a catch of sadness in her voice, "Poor old

Grandfather Stone! I suppose no one had kissed him for years. I remember the first night we were there Edwin kissed us good-night as he always did and then in the fullness of his warm little boy heart he went and kissed his grandfather on the cheek, and the old man looked so astonished I was afraid he would frighten the child. He never moved or said a word and his face did not change, and Edwin drew back, dashed. I was so sorry—sorry for them both."

So to be at home was not comfort for Andrew. It was only to return to the old inferiorities. Nevertheless, it was Andrew out of all the sons who, in his furlough, helped his father to collect his rents from lazy tenant farmers upon the place and put his accounts in order, Andrew who re-roofed the enormous old barn and painted the house and mended the stairs. Duty drove him as ambition or love or pleasure might drive another man. He never shirked what he hated, if he once saw it his duty. For God had said, "Honor thy father and thy mother." Sternly and with grim patience he honored them.

But there were times when Andrew could find the satisfaction for which his soul thirsted. He was sent to preach in churches for missions. He did not preach often in city churches to proud people, smartly dressed, who wanted a condensation of China's needs into half an hour. Andrew went to country churches, where people were not hurried, and where they expected something long enough to be worth putting on their Sunday clothes for, and driving a long distance over rough dirt roads. Farmers and their wives listened peacefully to the stories Andrew had to tell of sin and misery, comfortably aware that they themselves had no sin and very little misery. After he had finished they did not look at the clock, and they put a little into the collection, and somebody always asked him home to dinner.

Those dinners! Remembering them in after years Andrew would exclaim with a sort of accusing pleasure, "Such waste! Fried chicken and cold ham, beaten biscuit, four or five kinds of vegetables and potatoes, salads and preserves and pickles, and pounds of cake and pudding and like as not ice cream! It would have served the Lord better to have put more in the collection plate and less in their stomachs!"

But then Andrew kept his horror of self-indulgence. He loved good food as well as any man, but he would not eat more than he thought necessary for strength to do God's work. The rarer the dainty, the more stern he was to refuse all or more than a morsel. Plain food, eaten slowly and sparingly, was his rule. And yet his innocent pleasure in a cup of tea on a cold afternoon, in a bowl of hot soup at supper when the day's work was over, was as keen as any gourmet's at the sight of terrapin or caviar or any useless and delicious food. The result of doing his duty was of course that he lived to eighty as strong and spare as an oak, and when his flesh was washed for burial it was as smooth and fresh upon his body, below the strong dark sunburn of face and neck, as any child's could be.

He recorded little of those two years in his own country. They stayed the two years sorely against his will, because Carie was with child and she had refused to go back until the child was born. He would have persisted and won except that Carie's father, that man whose stature was the stature of a little man, but whose soul was the soul of Hercules, and more bold, reminded him of his three dead children.

"This child shall be born under my roof," he decreed. So Andrew waited with Carie in her old home, impatient to save other souls already born, until this small soul appeared. It was a girl, not quite worth waiting for. Andrew never made any bones about that. Years later when the child was grown and began writing books, Andrew was not impressed. Novels—they were worthless, a waste of God's time even to read, much less write. He picked up one of hers once, a thick volume, and glanced at it, and turned a leaf or two, and closed it. "I think I won't undertake that," he remarked with his habitual vague gentleness, and not in the least meaning to be unkind. Once he said, in duty, "I hope you never write anything not true, daughter," but he did not wait for her answer. It did not matter what the answer was. If he had spoken, his duty was quite finished.

Andrew never pretended he liked daughters as well as sons. His daughters existed, as his wife did, to take care of him. This, if he had been aware of his selfishness, they might have found difficult to bear. But he was not in the least aware of it. He was as touchingly, as confidingly, selfish as a little child. He looked to wife and daughters naïvely for all material things, taking for granted the comforts of food and proper clothing, warmth and light and all that he wanted for home. Once when he was an old man, or nearly old, and Carie was gone and he was dependent for these things upon a daughter who was herself a mother, a wife and bread-winner to boot, he fell very ill, and after a few days of incessant nursing when he would have no one but his daughter near him, the doctor compelled him to go to a hospital. He was very sad and miserable, having no confidence in strange women. "I want to go home," he said the third day. "I have a daughter at home who has nothing to do but take care of me." It was what daughters were for.

But when he was young he did not need them, and he was in haste to be about God's business. Once again he bade his home and his parents good-by. But this time it was not in doubt and ignorance of what was ahead. He was in the full strength of his maturity and confidence.

He knew to what he was going, and he was sure of himself now, as well as of his mission.

He was never to see home or parents again. When, years later, he returned once more, they were dead, the obstinate placid old woman and the domineering high-spirited old man, who declared before he died, "God's cheated me! I begat seven sons and I haven't one left to live on the land," and so went grumbling into eternity. As for house and lands, they were sold at a bargain, and when the price was divided between seven sons and two daughters, there was only a pittance for each. They had chosen one brother to do the selling for all, and when he had done it, they railed at him for being a bad business man—all except Andrew who, ten thousand miles away, cared nothing. He took his pittance and put it into his New Testament. But then Andrew, like all his brother sons of God, was a very bad business man, too.

VI

WHEN Andrew's feet touched Chinese soil, he changed. Anyone seeing him in his own country would never have recognized him in China. In his own country he appeared a little ridiculous—a tall thin figure in ill-fitting garments made by a Chinese tailor, his prophetic head stooping on his gaunt shoulders, his eyes doubting and bewildered. On shipboard he appeared to smarter looking passengers as the missionary of story books, absorbed in his mission, mingling with no one. Not that he cared what they thought of him! He came and went among them, oblivious of them. It did not occur to him, I think, that ship's passengers had souls. Certainly women had not. He saw their frivolities with strong disfavor. But then he was one man whom no woman could blandish. Once on board ship he sat on deck reading a Chinese book, seeing nothing that was going on. It happened that a collection was being taken at the time among the passengers to buy prizes for some sports, and a committee of pretty women had been chosen to do the soliciting. Evidently they considered Andrew difficult. I saw them arguing among themselves, throwing glances in his direction, to which he was completely impervious. Suddenly the prettiest and gayest said, boasting, "I'll do it! I've never had a man say no to me yet!" She sallied forth and putting on her very bewitching smile, she sat herself down on the arm of Andrew's chair, and began, coaxingly.

What she said no one ever knew. For Andrew gave her a look like the wrath of God and rose in mighty dignity and strode down the deck, his coat tails flying. But then he never looked at any woman. I used to complain to him that he never recognized my friends, and indeed that he passed his daughters on the street without speaking to them. To which he replied gently and firmly, "I never look a lady in the face. I consider it rude to do so."

By ridicule and contempt he was totally unmoved, for the simple reason that it did not occur to him to consider what people thought of him. Had their laughter been pointed out to him, he would not have cared. "What can man do to me?" he used to say. The world was divided into those who would be saved and those who would not. Those who would not were already lost and not to be heeded as alive any more.

It must be confessed that into this latter category he put most white men and all white women. "They have the means of salvation," he used to say, "and they do not take it." He was thinking of the churches in every town and village in his country. But I think he felt about souls very much as some people feel about eggs—he wanted them brown, and a brown one was worth any number of white ones. So far as I know he never endeavored to save the soul of a white man or woman, not even his own children. Certainly he never said a word to us on the subject of religion. Night and morning he held a simple form of prayers in his home for us, at which he did no preaching. He read a chapter from the Bible, heard us, when we were small, recite a verse apiece, and then he prayed.

When he prayed he became transfigured by his own belief. I have heard many men pray carelessly or fulsomely or for the ears of men rather than to God. I have seen them reading prayers aloud, openly or secretly, prepared prayers. But Andrew, when he prayed, did so with utter intense sincerity. He never opened his mouth and began to talk. He began always with silence, a moment, two moments, as many as he needed, to realize himself in the presence of God. Over his face would come a deep and solemn tranquillity. We felt him no longer among us. Then, his very voice changed, deepened, full of reverence, he addressed God and with him drew us, too. He never, in all the thousands of times I heard him pray, asked for any material benefit, except, in case of illness, for the sick one's recovery if it were in accordance with God's will. His prayers were always for the soul, for further understanding of God and duty, and the strength to do God's will. Even grace before meat was, after thanks, "Bless this food to our use and us to thy service, forever, amen."

So Andrew did not hear laughter or see ridicule. He was safe in the sanctuary of his own soul. But when he stepped upon the Chinese shore, he no longer had the air of a foreigner that he had in his own country. He was home again, not home in a physical sense so much as home in his place, in his work, in the fulfillment of life. Happiness was in his look, in the unwonted eagerness of his step and voice, in his impatience to be out of Shanghai and back in the interior among the common people whom he had come to save. All the paternal instincts of his heart went out to those who were his flock. His children never felt that warmth, but it was there—any Chinese soul in search of God could feel that priestly fatherliness in Andrew. He could be as gentle, as persuasive, as brooding over a soul as any father over an earthly child. He went back to them gladly, and they gave him the honor he never found in his own country.

There was therefore no strangeness in that return. He took passage upon a Yangtse River steamer and upon its deck piled the box of books he had brought back, the boxes of fresh tracts he had bought in Shanghai, and boxes of cheap writing paper, for he had already in mind a new task which was to occupy the rest of his life. Among the boxes was the round-backed trunk in which his wife Carie had packed her trousseau ten years before, and his own smaller round-backed trunk. But Carie's trunk held children's clothes now, too, and a little stock of needles and pins and thread, bits of lace and wool, all the small things which women need to make small garments, and which were not to be bought in the streets of a Chinese city. They all walked across the narrow gangplank, Andrew and his son Edwin and Carie carrying her baby daughter, then four months old. And once again they marched upon the heart of China.

Some of the most redoubtable battles that Andrew ever fought were upon those Yangtse River steamers. They were small, stockily built vessels, for the most part built in England, and their polyglot crews were headed by blasphemous, roaring, red-faced old English captains who had rampaged along the Chinese coasts for years and had retired into the comparative safety of the river trade. Not one of those captains but was full of tales of the pirates of Bias Bay and of bandits along the shores of the river, and they all had one love and one hate. They loved Scotch whiskey and hated all missionaries. Andrew was unmistakably and proudly a missionary, intrepid in independence, afraid of no man, and meat for any self-respecting captain. The fray usually began with some insult tossed out by the captain, for Andrew was always quiet and apparently gentle in demeanor. The favorite insult had to do with the obscenity in the Bible. The captain would proclaim in a loud hearty voice to his mate, "Fact is, it beats me how these missionaries can hand around a book like the Bible. It's got more dirty stories in it than you can find in any other book. Corruptin' the heathen, that's what it is!"

A dark red would begin to creep up out of Andrew's collar.

"You seem to know certain parts of the Bible very well, Captain," he would remark.

"You can't deny it, can you?" the captain retorted.

Andrew, lifting his piercing blue eyes to the captain's face, replied with the immense tranquillity that we all feared when we heard it. "The Bible, it is true, has certain accounts of sinful men and how God dealt with them. They were punished for their sins. He who reads aright, reads to the salvation of his soul. But there are those who read to their own damnation." And he would help himself serenely to the inevitable rice pudding and stewed prunes of the ship's fare.

Sometimes the fight went no further than a snort from the captain. But if it went on, Andrew fought it to the end with great pleasure and without animosity. It was only in the very lean years a little later, when the printing of his New Testament was eating up all we had, that he escaped the duels with the river captains, and then because we could not afford to travel upstairs with other white people. We put on Chinese clothes and traveled below decks with the Chinese. Andrew took advantage of the enforced congregation then, and went among them with his tracts, preaching and talking. They listened to him willingly enough, those who were not smoking opium or gambling, because there was nothing to do. They listened, yawning aloud with boredom, as he told them fervently how Christ died for their sins. They did not know what he meant by sins, or who this man was who wanted to save them, or why he did. They stared, half-listening, dropping to sleep in grotesque attitudes upon the deck, where they sat leaning against their bundles.

As for me, beginning then to see and feel, to perceive without knowing, I can never forget the smells of those ships. For we were come into the lean years as early as my memory goes, and I remember the darkness of the square low-ceiled saloons. They were always the same. At one side was the huge opium couch of wood and rattan with a long low table to divide it. There were always two drowsy figures outstretched, their lamps smoldering upon the table, and the thick foul sweetish fumes rising and creeping into every cranny. From the half-opened doors of the tiny cabins came the same smell, so that the close air seemed swimming with it.

Almost as large as the couch was a big round table upon which meals were served twice a day, but every moment otherwise it was used for gambling. Early in the morning the click and clatter of bamboo dominoes began, and it went on at night until dawn. The table was always crowded with players, their tense faces fierce with eagerness over the game. In the middle of the table was a pile of silver dollars which everyone watched covetously, closely, with terrible longing. The pile dwindled and grew, but occasionally it was swept away by a single lean dark hand. Then a strange growl went over the crowd of gamesters and over the crowd of onlookers always pushing one another around the table. They would not have stopped even to eat except that the dirty stewards swept the dominoes ruthlessly to the floor and set wooden buckets of rice upon the table and clapped down four or five bowls of cabbage and fish and meat, and bowls and bamboo chopsticks. In the same grim silence in which they had played they ate, bowl after bowl, searching in silence for the best bits of meat and vegetables. When the passengers were satisfied the stewards and cabin boys, all dirty and all insolent, gobbled up the remains.

But Andrew was imperturbable. He took his bowl and filled it sparely with rice and cabbage and went to the deck and stood eating, looking away from the grimy multitude, out to the smooth green banks of the river. He had a way of maintaining himself intact wherever he was, and people gave way to him in a sort of astonishment because he was continually in places where one did not expect to see such a figure as his, moving with dignity among the mean.

But he was always quite at home anywhere. No magnificence could awe him nor any poverty daunt him.

He slept peacefully in the dirty upper berths of the vile little cabins. In the lower berth with Carie I remember seeing his large bare feet protruding far beyond the end of the berth above. They were always too short for him, those berths, and he used to take turns resting his feet or his head, for as he remarked, he couldn't sleep both ends at once. But he never complained, having chosen what he wanted to do.

As for Carie, she spent her time keeping the children as antiseptic as possible with carbolic lotion and watching that their possessions were not taken from them. For the river ships were full of professional thieves. When they became so great a pest that business was lessened because of them, the owners of the vessels paid the thieves' guild a certain sum of money to stay off the ships for a while. But there were always some and they were very skilful at abstracting whatever they wanted. Once Andrew came back into the little cabin and Carie's sharp eyes spied an emptiness about his vest.

"Your watch is gone!" she exclaimed.

It was indeed, and a few minutes later when Andrew had need of his fountain pen, that was gone, too, and he felt for his purse and it was gone. While he had been out in the crowded saloon preaching, some clever-fingered thief, pressing close in apparent zeal to hear, had taken everything. Andrew looked stricken for a moment, especially over the pen, which was a gift and dearly prized and much used.

"Oh, pshaw!" he exclaimed.

It was as near as he ever came to "damn" and it meant the same thing and he always felt better after he had said it. But nothing cast him down for long. He was an invincible optimist, being always sure he was doing God's will, and therefore that everything would be all right in the end.

Back in the interior city where they had lived before, Andrew found no great welcome from his fellow missionaries. He found that his furniture had been cast carelessly out of the house which Carie had made into a home. Everything had been put into an outhouse, and the white ants had reduced his goods to nothing. "I took up my bookcase," he said solemnly, "and it fell into dust." Worst of all, his few precious books were ruined with mildew. He never quite forgave or forgot that. "I had a good commentary of the Bible," he used to say, remembering, pain in the memory. "I tried to paste the good bits onto separate sheets of paper."

There was some discussion over the house, now occupied by others. "We thought you weren't coming back," the other missionary said, excusing himself.

"Not coming back!" Andrew exclaimed. "I don't believe it!"

Then the story came out, bit by bit. He was, he was told, heretical in his views. He believed too much in human knowledge—else why did he spend time in educating his pastors? Why did he not, as the other missionaries did, trust to the inspiration of the Holy Ghost? Christ took ignorant men and made them his chief apostles. Indeed, they felt so strongly about it that they had written to the home board and to the supporting churches urging that he not be retained because of his unsound views. Andrew listened grimly until they had had their say. Then he told them what he thought of them.

"What did you say?" we asked in after years.

"I told them they were lazy," he said. "I told them they wanted to live in comfortable houses and to care for their own families and pamper their own bodies. I told them they were not worthy of their high calling. In short," he said with energy, "I told them they were hypocrites."

"Father!" we breathed.

"Oh, I said it all very kindly," he said peaceably.

But the upshot of it was that they told Andrew he might go where he liked and they would vote that he be allowed to do so. He always ended the story by saying triumphantly, "They cast a vote of confidence in me and gave me the money to open a new station wherever I liked."

He was too guileless of soul to see what they had really

done. They wanted to be rid of him at all costs—rid of his indefatigable energy, to be rid of his undying determination to be worthy of the calling which to him was holy, to be rid of his singleness of heart in his duty. Most of all they wanted to be rid of his sympathy for those whom he had come to save. He grew to love greatly the Chinese. It was a complaint against him that if the choice were given him to believe a Chinese or a white man, he always believed the Chinese. "I've learned bitterly that I can trust them more," he used to retort, grimly. He was rewarded by their devotion to him, and this did not make him better loved by his fellows. The truth was that Andrew was completely intolerant of the policies of missions. It was the policy of the missionaries to stand together at all costs against the "natives." If any individual missionary had a clash with a convert or a Chinese preacher, all the missionaries upheld the white man, regardless of right or wrong. "It wouldn't do," it was often said, "to allow the natives to undermine the authority of the missionary." For then what would become of the authority of the church?

But Andrew would sweep such talk aside with a gesture of his great hand. "Oh, pshaw!" he would say. He had no reverence for any human authority whatever. "There's the right of a thing," he used to say. And many a humble Chinese pastor, struggling in a little village church at ten dollars a month, had Andrew to thank that he had even so small a place of security. That miserable wage! Andrew battled for wages all his life—though never for his own. And when he could get nothing he squeezed out a dollar or two himself for the man who had been refused.

Yes, they wanted to be rid of Andrew's intolerance of race superiority and priestly authorities. "A prince of the church!" he used to say. "Oh, pshaw—there's no such thing possible!"

So he packed his few remaining books and Carie packed everything else and they went northward again into a new city.

There was no home to be rented in this city. No one would rent to the foreign devils. The best that Andrew could do was to find three small rooms in an inn so poor that the opium-smoking landlord was willing, being hard-pressed by his hunger for the drug, to let him have them at a high rent, since he had no guests anyway. The rooms were earthen floored, and the windows were very small, mere holes in the mud walls. But once a roof of any sort was over his family's heads, Andrew let it go at that and hurried to his own business.

And now it seemed to him he had never had a greater opportunity. For hundreds of miles he was the only missionary, the only white man. There were no other denominations with their interfering teachings. He had to himself an area as large as the state of Texas, full of souls who had never heard the Gospel. He was intoxicated with the magnificence of his opportunity.

But he had not come away alone. By now wherever he went there were some who followed him, Chinese preachers who chose him and his ways. Chief among them always was the tall Mohammedan, Ma, whose Arab blood was so clear in his thin haughty face and in his proud bearing. With this man and the few others Andrew planned his new campaign. The field—he always called the area for which he felt himself responsible his field—was drawn out upon a map, and a certain part apportioned to each for surveying. For Andrew must always know the material aspects of his fields—how many walled cities there were, and how many souls lived within the walls, and how many temples there were and what religion they belonged to, and what the chief business of each city was, and whether people lived well or poorly. These walled cities were to be the centers. Then he must know how many walled villages there were, and how many market towns, and where the chief tea houses were where farmers from the lesser villages gathered after they had sold their produce and had time to linger and listen. His goal was a church in every walled city and a chapel in every market town. But there was never any force about this. He always used to say proudly, "I never established a church or a chapel in a place where people did not want it."

"How did you know whether they wanted it or not?" we asked him when we were old enough to be wicked.

"They always did want it after I talked to them and told them what it meant to refuse God," he said.

What Andrew never knew was that one religion more or less meant nothing to the people. There was always the possibility that there might be an extra god somewhere of whom they had not heard, and whom they should propitiate for benefit. To add a white man's god could do no harm. Buddha himself had been a foreigner, though black. It was only when Andrew preached boldly that his god was the one true god that hostility arose. It was when Andrew told men that they must leave the worship of ancestors in their family halls because to bow before a man was to give what belonged to his god only, that many went away and ceased to follow him. But Andrew was never daunted. He had the faith that those whom God had called would remain, and those not predestined to remain would go away, and he let them go, unmoved.

Nevertheless, Andrew at this time of his life certainly set himself to the winning of souls. For one thing he put on Chinese garments and let his hair grow long and braided it into a queue. This was because his tall body and his foreign looks were terrifying to country people. Sometimes when he went into a village the whole population fled across the fields, leaving only the yellow dogs to bark at him. But he was never at home in Chinese robes. His long legs would get entangled and he grew impatient at once. "Oh, pshaw!" he would mutter and tuck the robes into his girdle as a coolie does. The long hair was especially intolerable and after much groaning and endurance he cut it off and bought a false queue which Carie sewed firmly inside his round black satin Chinese cap. It was not a bad imitation and freed him from the outrageous business of combing tangles out of his hair—it was not a bad imitation until he took his cap off, as he did everywhere, and hung it up on the wall. Then the effect of the queue was odd, to say the least.

But the Chinese costume did not last long. The loose sleeves and flying skirts soon became intolerable. Andrew liked his clothes buttoned tightly about him, and above all, he liked them plain. The silks of a Chinese gentleman he would not wear because they were too fine, and the cotton clothes of a poor man were limp and hung so grotesquely upon his huge frame that Carie refused to let him wear them. So he went back to his own garments after a while.

Andrew hated anything pretentious or strange in apparel. He scorned mightily the robes of the professional priest; nothing infuriated him more than a bishop's costume and he particularly scorned a clerical collar. "Nobody knows where they button," he used to say. "They slip on like a halter, maybe." Then he would add, with a touch of characteristic grimness, "A man oughtn't to need a uniform to show he serves the Lord God. It ought to be apparent in all he says and does."

He stoutly refused to wear anything but a plain business suit. He did own a Prince Albert, unwillingly bought for his own wedding, and some of the rousing scenes between him and Carie were over the wearing of this coat. Carie sometimes won by coaxing and a touch of flattery.

"You're tall enough to wear a long coat, Andy. Tall men look so nice in them."

Andrew was more susceptible even than most men to a little flattery from Carie—he had never been quite able to forget Mrs. Pettibrew—and he more often than not capitulated only to come home bitterly complaining of the discomfort of sitting on his tails.

"You shouldn't sit on them," said Carie. "Divide them, and sit between them."

But Andrew pshawed.

"I can't have my mind on such things in the presence of Almighty God," he retorted.

So the Prince Albert turned green with age and he would never buy another. Instead he went about obliviously in the cheap suits the Chinese tailors made for him. Yet he had his own curious formalities. He would never take off his coat in the presence of a lady, or on the hottest day sit down coatless to a meal. Nor would he ever wear any but white shirts and stiff winged collars, always very clean. He never looked himself without those collars. If one caught him, collarless, wrapped in his dressing gown on his way down the hall to or from his bath, his neck rose a little too thin for the large and nobly shaped head. It gave him a curious childlike and helpless look. One was glad to have him put the collar on again, because without it that childlikeness in him was exposed and he was somehow betrayed.

And he had that quality of childlikeness. He was always easily deceived. There was not a shred of shrewdness in him. He believed happily, for instance, everyone who came to him saying that he wanted to turn Christian. Andrew was incapable of distrusting any convert, or of questioning anyone who said he believed on the Lord Jesus Christ. It would have been to distrust Christ himself, for he thought one who believed was predestined to be saved, and he received each professing soul with a deep and touching confidence.

At a baptismal service Andrew was an amazing experience for anyone who saw him. Four times a year he received converts. They gathered in the chosen center, coming in from all over the field, a small crowd of simple country folk for the most part, but with a scattering of townspeople and, rarely, one who looked learned or a man of place. Andrew did not receive them lightly or baptize them at once. They stayed for as long as a week sometimes, while he taught them and examined them in their knowledge of the new religion. For weeks and even months before, his assistants had been teaching them, those who could not read to read the simple tracts Andrew had prepared for them, the others the Scriptures themselves. When they came up for baptism Andrew questioned each one carefully, both as to knowledge of the principles of Christianity and spiritual experience. Sometimes when ignorance was too blatant, he regretfully bade them go home and prepare further and come up again. But when there was earnest profession of belief he received them. In the church, before the congregation, they came up, one by one, and he called their names, and dipped his fingers in the plain pottery bowl he held, and sprinkling their heads, he prayed, thanking God for every soul thus given to him.

The expressions upon the faces of the baptized varied from terror to hopefulness. Often there was the look of those who searched sincerely after God. But as often there was the look of a smug and pious rogue. Nevertheless Andrew received them all as precious, and after they were baptized, he gave them communion. What they thought of the whole proceeding varied according to the sincerity of their purpose. There were those who declared publicly, as soon as the water touched their heads, that they felt as if a stone had been taken away from the door of their hearts, and there were those who said privately that they felt nothing at all, and could notice no change in life whatever, and it was a hoax.

But none of them mattered. What mattered was that on those days Andrew's soul touched ecstasy. He was literally transfigured with a joy not of this earth. He came home to Sunday dinner looking as though a lamp were burning brightly within him. He was not gay—his joy was too deep for that. He sat quietly, eating in his sparing way, not hearing anything that was said around the table, but there was a luminescence about him. I used to look at him and be sure I saw a pure pale light standing around him as though it came from his body. His eyes were particularly pellucid and blue. After dinner he invariably shut himself in his study for many hours, to emerge at last in a happy exhaustion.

Because of such hours, which none of us shared, indeed which no one could share with him, that study was like no room in the house to us. We never thought of playing there or indeed even going into it for any reason except to take him a necessary message. Later on I used to have to go there for him to hear my Latin lessons, and I never stood up to recite to him—and not to stand was unthinkable—without feeling that more than man was listening.

Out of that new field the converts came in like homing birds. It was a poverty-stricken region, plagued by famine, for the Yellow River wound its wilful way through those plains, shifting its bed, drying up one course to flood another. The people were angry with their own gods and weary with suffering, and one heard it often said, "No god can be worse than ours! Let us try the foreign god and see if any good comes of it!"

Some good came to a few, for Andrew and Carie got together food, begging money from home and the home churches, and relieving what distress they could. The people, eagerly hoping for far more than was in Andrew's power to give, crowded into the chapels, clamoring to be saved. When they found there could not be enough for all, many went out again, and yet some stayed, so that Andrew was greatly encouraged.

He was away from home continually, preaching and teaching. With him went his band of followers, whom he was training into a Chinese clergy. In each center as it was established he put a trained man to preach and to conduct a school. For Andrew loved learning, and wherever he put a church he put a school, too, where for a small sum the children of church members or any others could come and learn to read and write and be taught the principles of the Christian religion. If for reading they read the classics of Confucius, it did not disturb him. There was a magic in the Scriptures which could not be overcome by heathen literature. Thus he believed.

In the midst of all this success and growth he was struck a blow. It came from a point at which he could least have expected it. He came home one day from a long preaching tour. It was early spring and he had been away many weeks. Now he felt he had earned a week at home. It had been a wonderfully good tour. Everywhere he had been heard eagerly, and many had wanted baptism. Now, happy to his heart's core, filled with the knowledge of success in the work and of the consciousness of God's blessing, he let himself think of the pleasure of a hot bath and a clean bed, of good food, of the pleasure of speaking his own tongue—it had been long since he had heard or spoken English—and of seeing his family. He deserved a holiday—he could enjoy for a little while without a sense of guilt in enjoyment.

But when he entered the courtyard of the inn and got down from his donkey there was Carie, waiting for him —not only Carie but the three children—a son had been born not many months before—and the children's nurse. They were dressed for travel, and all the household goods were packed into loads ready to be carried by waiting men.

"Why—why—" Andrew gasped, stammering, "what does this mean, Carie?"

"It means," she replied, "that I and the children are going to find a place where we can live. You can preach from Peking to Canton, but I and these little children will never go with you any more."

I know that speech of hers by heart, because she said it to me so many times in telling it. And she knew it by heart because she had said it so many times in the weeks that Andrew had been away. She said it over and over when she was nursing the baby through pneumonia, with the water flooding into the rooms so that the furniture had to be put up on bricks and they walked about on planks laid like gangways from room to room. Hers had not been the joy of saving souls and preaching to the crowding multitudes. Bit by bit she had saved one life, the small life of her baby son—if indeed she had saved it, because he was still so frail.

I do not know exactly what took place there in that courtyard. Andrew always looked grim when he came to that point. "She was utterly beyond reason," he would say. For neither of them was it a struggle between a man and a woman. It was a woman defying God. She fought against God, against Andrew's call, against the success of his work, against the promise of the future.

"She did not care a whit for all the souls yet to be saved," Andrew said once in the bitterness of remembering. "She was like a wild wind—nothing could stop her."

In the end she won, as she had determined and planned to do. The rooms were empty, the landlord paid, the carts engaged and waiting to take them to the junk already hired. She had closed every door behind her. Andrew need not come, she told him—she could go alone. But he went with her, bewildered, angry, protesting. He turned for a moment to his comrade, Ma, and hastily promised to come back the instant he could settle his family somewhere. But he was greatly shaken. From within his own home a blow had been struck at him. He never quite forgave Carie for it, and from that day he went more solitary than he had before.

But then Andrew was born a solitary. He never had an intimate friend. When he was young he needed none. He had his dreams of escape from the labor he hated, and his plans for learning and his mission. Even when he was married he had no thought of companionship, for he had not seen a woman companion to a man. Among men he heard a crude scorn of women as creatures full of notions and whimsies, necessary to man and to be respected only in the simple functions of mating and housekeeping, and this scorn was slacked only by the brief aberration of courtship, to be resumed once it was over. It did not occur to him to look for or desire intellectual companionship or spiritual understanding in a woman. Occasionally, it is true, a woman was misled by a certain benignity in Andrew's look and by the quiet certainty of his manner and was drawn to him, and she made a sign to him of her interest. Nothing distressed Andrew more deeply or embarrassed him more profoundly. There was once at the breakfast table when, examining his mail, a look of shock spread over his face as he read a letter he had just opened. He handed it at once to Carie. She read it in a twinkling, her dark eyes firing with anger.

"The woman's a fool!" she said in her downright fashion. "You leave her to me—I'll answer that letter, Andrew!" She folded it and put it in her pocket. Then she glanced at him sharply. "You didn't go talking to her alone or anything like that to put ideas in her head?"

A clear sweat stood out on Andrew's high beautiful brow. He shook his head, too agitated to speak. Then he cleared his throat. "Wait a minute," he said hoarsely. "She asked me to talk with her a few minutes one night—I remember Mr. Jones was called out. She did not grasp fully the significance of St. Paul's conception of salvation by grace, and I explained it to her."

"And then she thanked you and said she had never understood it so well before!"

"How did you know?" he asked amazed.

Carie gave her short musical laugh. "I know how women get around men—they always begin by wanting advice on something or wanting something explained! Don't bother any more about it. I'll attend to her."

Andrew finished his breakfast in silence and went away, at once relieved and slightly sheepish. Immediately after breakfast Carie sat down at her desk, and wrote swiftly for a few moments. "There!" she exclaimed, addressing an envelope. "Poor silly soul!" She laughed, restored to good humor. Then she added, "Of course I knew Andrew was as innocent as a lamb! But that's always the kind that get taken in."

I don't believe she ever fully trusted Andrew about women because he was so guileless. When she lay on her deathbed, in her anguish and anger because she loved life, she said something bitter about his marrying again soon. And he came away, hurt. "She seems to think I'm—I'm—an old Abraham!" I heard him mutter down the hall. But it was not that. I think she knew she had never penetrated to that fastness of his heart where he lived alone, and so she was doubtful and wondered half sadly and half bitterly if perhaps another woman might enter where she had not.

What she never realized was that no one could enter there. Andrew did not know how to open the door to anyone. There were times as he grew older when he longed to have someone come in, when he hungered to feel someone close to him, but no one could come close, because he did not know how to let anyone. He kept his soul guarded and his heart closed. A caress, even from one of his children, abashed him, and he could not respond to it and so they ceased to give it. They were grown before they realized that he was secretly pleased by such a sign of affection, and that a word of praise or approbation made the very tears start to his eyes sometimes. But people did not praise him easily because he was too shy to praise others, too afraid of seeming fulsome. In that childhood home of his there was much rude fun made among all of them, and only he was so sensitive as to brood over the thrusts and suffer. And then no one thought of praising anyone. It would result in sinful conceit. So he grew up with a tongue that could criticize but could not, whatever the impulse of his heart, shape itself to the softness of praise. When his children were little they did not love him for this, but when they grew up and he was an old man, with the transparencies of old age, they saw that under a different and a kinder creed this soul would have flowered into a mellower humor and a freer kindness. There was the love of kindness there, and the craving that a child has, kept through all the scores of years, for affection and understanding. But none of this could he express.

So he felt that Carie never understood him—it did not occur to him to wonder whether he understood her—and he said nothing to her. He took her and the children down the canal to the river and then he found an empty house upon a hill, and he left them there and went on his solitary way again.

But God comforted him.

VII

THOSE eight years before the Boxer Rebellion were the years of greatest danger in Andrew's mission. Since he never stayed in established places, but was always pushing out into new and unknown places, he often found himself among hostile people. The Chinese have always been distrustful of foreigners, not only foreigners from other countries but even people of their own nation from other provinces or regions. This is perhaps because each village and town has maintained itself for centuries as a separate locality. There has been almost no government from above or outside, and the clan feeling is very strong. In some places it was the usual custom to kill any stranger who came unexplained by burying him alive. It was the very common thing in a village, as it is today, to set the savage half-wild dogs upon any newcomer. Andrew went on, doing no more than carry a stout stick with which to beat off the dogs. And the dogs, soon discovering him to be unafraid and wary of their tricks at his heels, learned to leave him alone until he pushed on into stranger places. They are cowards, those dogs!

No one will ever know exactly what dangers he endured, because he never talked about them without a great deal of questioning and drawing out. Then in a few sentences he might tell a story that another would have made into a day's tale.

There was the time when he lay asleep upon the brick bed of an inn and awoke, conscious of a light, to find the innkeeper standing beside him, a bean-oil lamp flaming in his left hand and in his right a meat-chopper from the inn's kitchen. Andrew, opening his eyes, fixed them full upon the man's face and cried aloud to God.

"Deliver me, God!"

He spoke in English and the man grew afraid.

"What are you saying?" he asked.

"I am calling to my God," Andrew replied, never moving his steady blue eyes from the man's face.

The man lifted the meat-chopper firmly and brandished it. "Are you not afraid?" he shouted.

"No," said Andrew quietly. "Why should I be afraid? You can do no more than kill my body, and my God will punish you."

"How?" asked the man, pausing again.

"You will live in torment," said Andrew with such calm certainty that the man stared at him a while and went muttering away at last.

"What did you do then?" we asked Andrew, breathless.

"I turned over and went to sleep," he replied.

"He might have come back!" we breathed.

"There was a guard over me," he said simply.

Once he was pushed from a crowded ferry boat into a river by a rough fellow who first cursed him, and finding him unmoved, jostled him and tripped him over. But Andrew came up out of the muddy water and caught hold of the junk's rudder and held on. The crowd stared down at him, but not one offered him a hand. But he did not ask for a hand. He clung on until the river bank came under his feet and then he walked out, dripping wet, but imperturbable, to hunt for his box on the ferry boat. It was gone; the fellow had taken it.

The crowd laughed. "It was full of silver dollars," they cried. "All foreigners travel with boxes of silver dollars!"

Andrew smiled and went on his way content. His few silver dollars were safely in his pocket and the box had been full of tracts and Gospel sheets. "God has ways for men," he said in telling of it, and was convinced that the man's soul would be saved.

More than once he was laid upon and beaten when he appeared unexpectedly in some strange town. They beat him, apparently, for no reason except that they had never seen anyone like him before, as dogs will set upon a strange dog they have not seen.

But the things he really minded the most were not these. He was a fastidious saint physically, and he came home often quite ill with sickness at what he had had to endure of filth. Once he came in green with horror.

"What is it?" Carie cried.

"I have eaten serpent today," he said in a ghastly voice. "I ate it at an inn and did not know it until afterwards." And immediately he was sick with the thought.

The common custom of hawking and spitting he could not endure. He who was so infinitely patient with men's souls had no patience at all with their bodies. When the trains first began to run he rejoiced in the signs put up against spitting elsewhere than in the numerous spittoons provided. But no one paid any attention to the signs. The Chinese were accustomed to spit where they pleased. Most of them could not read, and those that could paid no heed. Physical convenience is the law of life in China. Andrew came home one summer evening looking very content.

"There was a great fat fellow on the train today," he said abruptly at the supper table.

We all looked at him, waiting.

"He had off his shirt and sat in his drawers and his belly was like a great frog's," he went on, disgust in his eyes. He wiped his mouth carefully. "He spat everywhere except in the spittoon. I could not bear it, and pointed to the sign."

"I hope it did some good," said Carie, skeptically.

"It did not and I told him what I thought of him," said Andrew.

"What did you tell him?" we asked.

"I told him he was filthier than a beast," Andrew said gently.

"Father!" we cried.

"Oh, I told him very kindly and pleasantly," he replied, in the same mild voice, and could not understand why we laughed.

He had, of course, enemies. Most of them, it is true, were among his fellow missionaries, but these he considered his natural enemies. Missionaries and magistrates he put in the same class as his enemies, that is, persons designed by the devil to thwart the will of God, or what he, Andrew, wanted to do. Magistrates he was ruthless toward, and he quite openly used every treaty right he had to force them to allow him to rent property for chapels. For though he never opened chapels unless there were those who wanted it, still there were always opposing groups who did not want the foreigner's religion in their town. These Andrew disregarded completely. If there were one soul who wanted to hear of God, it was that one's right to hear, though there might be a hundred who did not want to hear. So he went boldly to magistrates' courts, presenting himself again and again, waiting hours upon their whims. Sometimes a magistrate, not really meaning to see him at all, put him off from day to day with one excuse and another. Day after day Andrew presented himself at dawn to wait until night, only to come again, until everyone was weary with him.

Nor would he use the slightest touch of silver upon the palms of the underlings. He knew very well that money would have opened doors, but he had no money of his own and he would not so use the church's money which he held to be for the preaching of the Gospel alone. At last, if the magistrate proved obdurate, Andrew would use force—that is, the force of the treaties made after the Opium Wars by which Chinese citizens were to have the right to be Christian if they liked and missionaries the right to preach. If the magistrate were himself a doughty soul and would not be awed by treaties even with the threat of gunboats behind them, Andrew appealed to his own consul who, however he might curse missionaries—and how many of them do curse missionaries and groan, I suppose, very truly, that life would be simple without them!—would nevertheless be compelled to send an official letter to the magistrate. This letter, written upon official paper bearing the large strange seal of the unknown United States, always did what Andrew wanted. Grudgingly, in terms of carefully worded contempt, the permission would be given. But Andrew cared nothing for man's contempt. He went away to preach in triumph, being the stubbornest of the stubborn sons of God.

Well, all those years we at home scarcely saw Andrew, and to his children he was a stranger, coming home very seldom, and when he did, not as one who came home but as one who came only for a night's rest before he went on again. Their lives were built without him, their days filled with other presences than his. They were fatherless, because his life was dedicated to others, but they did not even know him well enough to miss him. He felt this vaguely, sometimes, when he came home and saw his son growing tall, and his daughter ceasing to be a little child, and the baby who had been born at the inn. But that one died when he was five, just before the last child, a girl, was born.

Sometimes he tried to enter into their lives. There were two times in the year when they remember him a little differently, not as a journeying angel who tarried with them a night, but as a man who shared the things they had to do. Of these two times one was Christmas and the other was when the boxes came from Montgomery Ward, and Christmas was really the less exciting.

For Christmas, of which Carie made so much for the children, was a somewhat doubtful occasion to Andrew. There had been no celebration of Christmas in his childhood home except going to church and having a dinner. There was no giving of gifts, no Santa Claus. His idea of gifts was strange, too. He could never think of things to give the children, except things he had wanted as a boy, and which they did not want. But if he did not know how to give gifts to his children, he knew less what to give Carie. Even the children felt the pain of an inadequate gift to her, and they knew enough to feel an ache in their hearts for her on Christmas morning when she opened a brown paper parcel and put it quietly aside without comment. But her eyes were shadowy. Yet we knew he meant nothing—only he never knew her, he did not know what she liked or what she wore or what she needed. The children, passionately adoring her, worked to give her what they could, spending weeks before Christmas to make "something pretty for Mother." They knew the secret craving of her heart for pretty things.

But of course Andrew, underneath all, could not bear the spending of money for anything that did not further the cause of his life. Money was the power to save souls—money to rent chapels, to open schools, to buy Bibles. He did not want anything for himself. So there was always a little ache about Christmas. And then he would murmur doubtfully, "No one knows the authentic date of Christ's birth. Besides, there is evidence that the festival is mixed with heathen traditions. We do not really know what we are celebrating—perhaps even the birthday of an ancient heathen god!"

"Fiddlesticks, Andrew," Carie exclaimed. "The point of it is to give the children a good time!"

But no one had ever troubled to give the child Andrew a good time, and he was more doubtful than ever. The truth is he was never free from the weight of his task. His happiness was measured by his success in that, and that alone. God had him.

But the Montgomery Ward boxes were another matter. They were necessities, ordered months before, paid for, and safely arrived. The children anticipated for weeks that morning when Andrew, looking up from the letters before him on the breakfast table, would say solemnly, "The boxes have come!" If he were not at home they could scarcely bear it, for Carie would not open them until he came. But he was nearly always there in the early winter. There was a regular routine to be followed, always exciting. Andrew must go down to the Customs office on the Bund and present the bill of lading and get the boxes through Customs. The children at home were waiting at the gate of the compound, if it were fair, climbing high so that they might catch the first glimpse of Andrew around the corner of the old Buddhist temple in the valley. If it were raining, they waited at the front door, their noses pressed white against the glass pane. Meanwhile Carie was preparing a place in the back hall for the boxes.

There was no greater ecstasy than the moment when Andrew appeared from behind the temple, followed by four or five coolies with boxes slung on ropes upon their carrying poles. The sound of their rhythmic step-keeping call floated up the hill and came nearer and nearer— "Heigh-ho—heigh-ho—" Soon, soon the boxes would be dropped in the hall, and the men clamoring about them in the dear confusion of the hour. Andrew would be waging a war over the tips the coolies were shouting for, slapping their sweaty breasts, pointing out the welts upon their horny shoulders.

"These foreign boxes are full of lead!" they would shout. "They are fit to kill us—and we came up the hill—and what is this mite upon my hand!" They would throw their coins down and spit upon them, and Carie would implore Andrew, "Give them a little more, Andrew—just this once!" And then very unwillingly he would give them a little more, and they would subside into grins and go away. And there were the boxes!

Some child always had the hammer and the big nail puller that Andrew had bought for such days, and breathless they watched while the strong iron teeth sank into the wood as Andrew pounded and clutched the nail head and the nail came up, screeching with reluctance.

Every board was saved as it came off, because the boxes were good American pine, dry as no wood in China was ever dry. All our bookcases and bureaus and the chests in the attic were made of the Montgomery Ward boxes. Under the lid was strong brown paper. Carie pulled it away, and there were the things from America! It was our most real, most tangible touch with our own country.

Now, looking back, the things seem very simple, such things as the Americans order every day from their grocers and think nothing but necessities. But to us they were the dearest luxuries, things that could be bought nowhere around us, foods to be tasted and savored and enjoyed as precious, tools that seemed magic in complexity, garments made and ready to wear, marvels of fashion.

But really there were tins of coffee and bags of sugar, cakes of yeast and soap, a round keg of molasses for Carie's famous gingerbreads, and spices which perhaps had grown in the Orient and now were back again ready to be used. There were needles and pins, hairpins and threads, all the small things not to be found in Chinese stores—some ribbon in gay colors to be used to tie back little girls' curls on Sundays (dyed tape on other days) and there were other little luxuries—sassafras tea, which Andrew loved on a cold winter's night at supper, and a few pounds of hard peppermint candy, some packages of gelatin, jars for fruits that Carie put up against the winter. For clothing there were the necessities of long underwear for the damp Chinese winters in badly heated houses—Carie knitted our stockings and sweaters and little cuffs she called wristlets. And last there was always a little special thing that each child had chosen out of the fabulous catalogue. Oh, the lovely hours we all spent poring over the catalogue, searching for the one thing, costing not more than the dollar we were allowed, the heart-burning decisions as to whether it were better to have several small things costing less or the one beloved thing costing a full dollar! And the agony when the one beloved cost a dollar and nineteen cents! There was no use in going to Andrew—no child thought of it—but Carie, always too tender-hearted, could be persuaded, and when the bill was presented to Andrew's stern eyes, Carie could be trusted to speak up and say, "I told her she could, Andrew—I'll make it up out of something else, or take it out of the housekeeping!" So Andrew let it pass—although to do him full justice he sometimes let it pass anyway, if the work were going well and he was in a high humor.

Each child, then, had his little package, precious to receive, precious to unwrap and to look at and fondle and play with and put under the pillow at night. Yet the catalogue was a book of heart-burning, too. So many things cost much more than a dollar! There was one of Andrew's little girls, for instance, who yearned deeply over years for a certain large baby doll. To this day she has not forgotten that doll. The legend underneath read "life-size." That meant as big as a real baby. She remembers its round bisque face in a frilly lace bonnet, its chubby hands, its long dress and little knit jacket. But it cost three dollars and ninety-eight cents and was of course hopelessly out of possibility. She bought a little doll or two, but they were never the same. She prayed resolutely for years that some Christmas—but there never was such a Christmas. She had little cheap dolls, dressed exquisitely and completely by Carie's hands. But they were not life-size. Every Christmas Eve that child, having prayed hundreds of prayers, went to bed with her heart beating with hope. But the first glance at the stocking and at the tiny heap of packages swept the hope away again for another year. If Carie had realized, she would have somehow seen to it, by some prodigious slashing sacrifice, that the small heart had its desire. But she never knew, for the child never spoke, not dreaming that the fabulous sum was within her parents' possibility to give. Santa Claus—or God—might give it, but not Andrew who needed all the money. And Carie had no money of her own. So the doll remained upon the pages of the catalogue to dream over and at last to relinquish, except to this day that child, now long grown, cannot pass the doll counter in a toy shop—cannot have her fill, for that matter, of real babies.

But there were many little white children living in the heart of China to whom Montgomery Ward took place with Santa Claus and God. One child came home one day to say solemnly to her mother, "I feel sure Miss Nan and Mr. Rob are going to be married."

"How do you know?" the mother inquired.

"Because I saw them looking at a Montgomery Ward catalogue together," the child replied, astutely.

All this time a slow storm was rising out of the deeps of China. None of us realized it, certainly not I as a small child living in Andrew's house. Yet I remember being afraid in the night because of things I heard Andrew and

Carie talk about. People were not as willing to hear Andrew preach as they had been, it seemed. He came home more often than he used to come, and very often he was dejected and downcast so that before he came Carie used to coax us to be especially good, to be affectionate with him and remember how tired he was.

"You children can't understand all the hard things he has to bear while you live safely here—" She paused, as though listening, wondering, perhaps, how safe the children were.

But they were warm-hearted little things and ran about doing things for Andrew's coming—picking flowers he never noticed, and putting his old leather slippers at the door for him to slip on when he came in—a thing he did notice and enjoy. There was a sort of symbolism in those large worn leather slippers, shaped to the angles of Andrew's feet. To a small child, carrying one in each hand, they seemed as enormous as a giant's shoes, and they had a sort of magic, too, because when Andrew put them on a different look came over his face. It was his home look—a desperate weariness of the body, a lightening of the heart, and a certain famishment in the eyes. But perhaps it was only eagerness for home and his own about him, an eagerness he was not able to put into words.

As the years went on which led to the Boxer Rebellion, he was more and more dejected when he came home. He spent hours sitting in his study, doing nothing, apparently. We used to see him sitting there in his old imitation leather armchair that he had picked up in a second-hand shop in Shanghai. It had, as long as I can remember, pieces of excelsior stuffing coming out of it, and spots where his body pressed upon it most hardly, especially in two spots where his elbows leaned when he prayed.

There was talk, too, because Andrew and Carie never hid the realities of their lives from their children. Andrew would say suddenly at the table, "I've had to close up three more chapels this last month. The landlords wouldn't let me keep them. I can't find another place—nobody will rent me a place to preach in now. Something's wrong."

Or he would say, "We're having meetings at the houses of different church members. We have to have them as the Christians did of old—at midnight, secretly, as we are able."

Many and many a night the children woke to hear the clang of the compound gate and to see the flicker of Andrew's big old kerosene oil lantern which he carried at night and kept spotlessly clean himself. It was one of his small fastidiousnesses—a clean lantern, or at home, the lamp clean and trimmed. For in those days we used oil lamps and American kerosene oil. When we saw the flicker of light upon the whitewashed wall, we knew that was Andrew coming home from a secret meeting of Christians.

The whole house came somehow to be filled not with fear but with a sort of solemn waiting. One by one the servants, on some pretext or another, left, until there were only the nurse and her son. And Andrew was at home more and more, his face growing daily more grim. He went several times to see the American consul and came back to say to Carie, "He can't do anything—they're all waiting."

And one night he never came home at all! It was nearly noon of the next day before he came in, and his wrists were bleeding where thongs had held him.

When Carie, frantic with anxiety, cried out, he answered soberly, "Be glad I am alive. I was at Lin Meng's administering communion to his old mother when soldiers came in. They took Lin away and tortured him until he died. But he remained true. They took his ten-year-old son, but let him go today, and he came back and told me and loosed me. I was left bound, and the woman died as I stood there, bound to a post." His face worked, and he sat down and groaned. Then he looked at us all strangely, his ice-colored eyes shining, his voice solemn and triumphant. "Lin Meng has entered into the presence of our Lord, a martyr, to stand among that glorified host!"

He got up quickly and went away into his study, to be alone a while.

So it was everywhere. For soon there began to come rumors of death. In one town in Shantung the small missionary community were all killed, including the children. Several times missionaries we had never seen before were brought to us by secret friends among the Chinese, ragged and starved and ill, and Carie cared for them and sent them on to Shanghai and safety. There were sometimes children of eight or ten with them, a very few, but never any little ones or any babies. These had died of dysentery, of fever, of hardships too dreadful to be told. The children of Carie never heard the rumors, but they saw Carie rock herself in weeping and anguish and fear for her own. So the storm mounted and mounted, until that day when the American flag raised at a point long agreed upon warned us to leave instantly, and Carie took the children and went. But Andrew stayed, alone.

It is not possible fully to know what was in Andrew's mind when he went back, the solitary white man in that whole countryside. Never, not then or after, did he leave his post when danger came. He went back quietly. On the way he was spat upon many times, and curses were shouted after him. But curses were common and he paid no heed to them. He entered the empty house, bathed and changed his clothing, and sat down to his supper.

One young lad, the son of the children's faithful nurse, remained to serve him.

The story of the Boxer Rebellion has been many times told and there is no use in telling it again. It remains, like the tale of the Black Hole of Calcutta, one of the festering spots of history. If the number of people actually dead was small, as such numbers go in these days of wholesale death by accidents and wars, it was the manner of death, the innocence of little children and babies, that makes the heart shudder and condemn even while the mind can reason and weigh. The mind can acknowledge the force of the Chinese right to refuse foreigners upon their soil, it can acknowledge the unwarranted imperialism of such men as Andrew, righteous though they were, and honorable in intent and of good meaning. The mind says people have a right to refuse imperialism. But the heart shudders. For those who were martyred were the good and the innocent, none the less good and innocent because they were blind. For the glory of God had made them blind. They were drunk with love of God, so that they saw nothing but His glory, could only see the one necessity, that all others should become like themselves. And so forsaking all else they went out as blind men do, trustful, not able to see danger, or if seeing, not believing.

There is no reconciling these two, the mind and the heart. The mind may say a thousand times, and rightly,

"They had no right to be there. They provoked what they received." But the heart answers, "They were innocent, for they believed that what they did was of God."

So there is no answer and there can be no just decision. Certainly Andrew belonged to the blind. It was his strength that he believed so deeply in what his soul said that the eyes of his flesh were never opened from birth until death. He never saw men except "as trees, walking." He would have been amazed if anyone had told him that the Chinese had the right to protest the presence of foreign missionaries upon their soil. It was as though they protested the actuality of the true God, his God. No man had any right against God.

He stayed stubbornly on in the square mission house with the one Chinese lad all through the hot brilliant summer. The lad, hanging about the streets at night, brought him rumors each day of new massacres of white people in other places. Andrew was the sole white man in the region. He came and went quietly, preaching openly in the streets until the fury of passersby and their shouts grew too threatening for him to be heard. Then with that high serene stubbornness of his he handed out his tracts, saw them dropped or torn, and went away to try in another street. His quietness, the extreme dignity of his tall figure, his lack of any fear seem to have preserved him. I know that from Ma, the Christian, who stayed by him still. Once he said to me of Andrew, "I thought many times that he would be killed. Many times I stood near, thinking I must, like Stephen, be witness to the death of a martyr. There were stones flung at him—once a stone cut him on the cheek, but he did not even put up his hand to wipe away the blood. He did not seem to feel it."

"Were you afraid?" we asked Andrew when he was an old man, remembering.

He considered. "There have been times in my life when I have been afraid. But it was always over small matters." He meant thieves, noises in the night, those stirs in the darkness which moved some childhood fear hidden in him so deeply that he did not recognize it. "But I never was afraid when I was on God's business," he said.

"Yet some were killed," we murmured.

"It is not death one fears," he said. It was one of his simplicities to which there was no answer.

But he was sustained in all those days so that afterwards he remembered with clarity, not dangers or fears, not stories of disease and death, but a sort of ecstasy. He lived, it seemed, outside himself.

"I seemed," he wrote, "without the body. For I was conscious of the presence of God with me like a strong light shining, day and night. All human beings were far away from me. I had almost no human intercourse except with Ma, once a Mohammedan, but now the Christian. He remained faithful. And every day I taught him exegesis of the scriptures, and together we planned for more effective spreading of the Gospel when the storm was abated."

For Andrew never doubted that the storm would abate, that evil must break down and good be triumphant. He prayed aloud in every prayer he ever made, "Keep us faithful until that sure day when evil is gone from the world and God is victorious." That sure day! Upon such surety he built his life, and being without doubt or shadow of turning, he lived happily in any circumstances. What more, indeed, does anyone need than the surety of his heart's wish?

Months went on. The summer ended, and the rebellion ended, as all the world knows, by a punitive expedition of the Powers from whom the slaughtered missionaries came. The foreign armies marched into Peking, the Empress Dowager fled with her court; apologies, indemnities, fresh concessions followed in the usual order. But the people remained sullen. They maintained a menacing refusal to hear anything about a foreign God. Andrew grew impatient. The cool weather came on, the sort of weather when he ought to be out over the country, preaching in sunny market-places, stopping in villages, talking to peasants gathered about the threshing floors. But they would not hear him. They threatened him, they set their fierce dogs upon him, they refused him room to rent or space even to stand. Twice a chapel was burned.

"God has not yet had time to work," Andrew wrote Carie.

It occurred to him that it had been nine years since he had seen his own country and that a furlough was due him. Carie, too, living in close rented rooms in Shanghai, was ready for a change. Well, he would give God a little more time, then. A year of furlough, and then he would come back, and he and the Christian Ma would begin their campaign again. He shut up the square mission house and went to Shanghai. His children had almost forgotten him, although every night they had prayed, "God, please keep our father from the Boxers."

He appeared taller than ever to them, thinner, and his eyes were hoary blue in the burned red-brown of his face. And he was shy with them and did not know how to talk to them.

VIII

OF that second return of Andrew's to America I can write with some authority because by then I can remember him on my own account. It is true I cannot yet give a consecutive story because my memory is not long enough for that. I see him not as a day to day figure, like Carie. The days came and went, and into them he broke irregularly and with violence. He must always have created a stir of some sort when he came, because those impressions of his presence are much more vivid than anything else, although a great deal was happening to me which had never happened before—all of America, in fact. I remember, for instance, my first glimpse of Cornelius, Carie's beloved brother, who had stood next to God all my life. He came out of the big white house in which Carie had told me I was born, his white hair glittering in the sun. He looked the oldest man in the world, and I thought he must be Hermanus, and I cried out, "Grandfather!" But Cornelius laughed, and behind him I saw still another older, more silver-haired figure, and that was Hermanus. Yet in all this excitement, in the excitement of cousins to play with, of an orchard heard of but never before seen, of cows and horses, of unwalled meadows—how strange and naked I felt at first with no wall to shield the house and garden, and then when I became convinced bandits would not attack us or anyone come in and steal our things, how glorious and free!

Yet upon all these memories Andrew's figure breaks in, in its own startling fashion. We stayed at Carie's home all summer and I was in a long ecstasy of happiness, day after day. Andrew was away visiting his own brothers and sisters—Carie, I think, felt them difficult to visit with two small, amah-bred children. And he preached at churches whenever he was invited. I remember my anxiety, when he was asked to preach in Carie's home church, that he would not be able to preach in English, and my amazement when he not only preached but preached very long indeed. He had, I felt, more than enough to say. That was the church where Andrew's brother David was minister, David who looked so much like Andrew that I was quite bewildered by it. But he was quieter than Andrew, paler and more gentle. He was a silvery pale old gentleman then, his very skin as pale as silver, so that he looked ghostly. Even the blue of his eyes was beginning to be dimmed by a silver film of rheum.

Andrew threw the family into consternation because he was so late in arriving the Saturday before the Sunday he was to preach. I felt quite miserable and somehow responsible for it. Hermanus kept watching and snorting about the delay and Carie kept apologizing, and I felt, since Andrew was my father, I ought to be able to do something about it. It was a hot August day and most of the afternoon I sat on the stile under the huge old maple, watching the dusty road. Around the supper table the aunts and uncles looked severely at Carie. "Is he usually late like this?" they inquired of her.

"No—no, indeed," she replied hastily. "I can't think what's keeping him. He wrote me he was riding horseback from Lewisburg today over Droop Mountain."

"He'll be worn out if he does get here now," Hermanus said gloomily and added, "He's not such a good preacher that he can get up and do us credit offhand."

Carie did not answer, though I saw a kindling in her eyes. I felt at once an odd aching—it was strange that she, my mother, should be scolded like a little girl, and I wanted to defend her.

Then suddenly Andrew walked in, his suitcase in his hand, his shoes very dusty.

"Well, sir!" cried Hermanus.

"My horse went lame when she'd gone less than two miles," said Andrew, "so I walked."

They all stared at him.

"Walked!" cried Cornelius. "Over Droop Mountain—and a bag!"

"There wasn't any other way to get here," said Andrew. "I'll just go and wash myself." He disappeared and I can still remember the clamoring and the astonishment. He had walked fifteen miles over a great mountain, carrying his suitcase.

I was suddenly very proud of him and piped, "There're always books in his suitcase, too!"

But Hermanus said grimly, "He'll be no good at all tomorrow." And when Andrew came in presently, very washed and speckless, he shouted to my Aunt Dorothy, "Go and fetch some hot meat! The man's famished!" and sat there, snorting a little from time to time while Andrew ate.

Whether or not Andrew was any good I do not remember, because the next morning after breakfast I suddenly announced my decision to join the church. It had not occurred to me until I saw my favorite cousin, just older than I, trying on a new white frock before breakfast. "I'm going to join the church today," she said complacently, turning around and around before the mirror. I stared at her, pondering. I also had a new white frock, ready for some occasion not yet arrived. Indeed, it had been a sore point between Carie and me that as yet there had been no occasion good enough. The idea struck me. I flew to Carie.

"I want to join the church, too!"

She was in her room, twisting up her heap of bright chestnut hair. She twined the coil in her hand, and looked at me in the mirror, her face very solemn.

"You can't just join the church like that," she exclaimed, outraged. "It's a very important step—you must think about it a long time."

"I have," I said quickly. "I've thought of it lots of times!"

"Then why didn't you say so before?" asked Carie shrewdly.

I twisted a bit of my frock. "I've always been afraid to go up alone," I said. "But today I could go up with Hilda."

Carie looked at me, thinking. "I don't know," she said finally. "You'll have to ask your father."

Andrew came in at that instant, his eyes tranquil from morning prayer.

"This child wants to join the church!" Carie cried.

I felt his eyes rest on me with more interest than I had ever felt in them. Indeed, except when I was in fault, I did not remember that they had ever turned full upon me before. But to one in fault they were piercing, terrifying. Now they were different. There was an eagerness of interest in them—they were almost, if not quite, kind.

"What makes you think you want to profess Christ?" he asked gravely.

I pleated my frock and said nothing, not knowing what to say. They stared at me. I could feel the two qualities of their stares. Carie's was shrewd and a little skeptical. A few more moments and she would be ready to forbid the whole business. But Andrew's gaze was softening, expanding, becoming exalted.

"You love the Lord Jesus Christ?" he inquired.

Suddenly there was nothing of father and daughter between us. He was the priest inquiring of a soul. Even I was awed and paused for a moment's searching. Did I not love Jesus? I had never thought about it, taking it for granted. He was, I had been told, kind to children.

"Yes, sir," I faltered.

He turned solemnly to Carie. "We have no right to forbid a soul's profession," he said.

"But the child's too young to know what she's doing!" Carie exclaimed.

I would not look at her, knowing the penetrating power of her dark and searching eyes. Besides, did I not love the Lord Jesus Christ?

"Of such is the Kingdom," said Andrew simply.

That settled it. Without a word, but her eyes still skeptical, Carie produced the white frock and I put it on and she tied the sash and adjusted my big leghorn hat, and we went to church. The family had been told of the situation, and my cousin and I walked side by side, behind Hermanus, feeling very special.

"You have to answer questions," Hilda whispered.

"I don't care," I whispered back. Had I not been nurtured on the Child's Catechism and the Westminster Shorter Catechism and hundreds of psalms and hymns?

It is true that at least a million times I had been pettish and complained to Carie, "I don't see what good all these catechisms and verses will do me!" To which she invariably replied, "The time will come when you will be glad of them." Perhaps, I pondered, this was the time—although I had never believed her.

That was why Andrew's sermon seemed so long. I did not listen to it, because I never listened to his sermons, feeling I could hear him talk any time at home. But being a shy child I began to wish I had not said I wanted to join the church. Now that it was inevitable, for Uncle David had been told, and it would never do to back down before all the family, my heart was throbbing in my throat like a dry and rasping machine. Only the thought of my frock upheld me. It was much prettier than Hilda's, and everybody would see it.

Of the rest I remember little. Before the benediction Uncle David rose and announced the receiving of two members, and invited all who would to remain after the benediction. Everyone remained. Carie slipped the hat from my head, and Hilda and I walked up the aisle together, an unending aisle, it seemed to me, although afterwards Hilda said I went so fast she had almost to run. I know I could feel my curls bobbing up and down against my back. There was a moment of complete silence, and then Uncle David's silvery blue eyes looked into mine and he asked a question or two, to which I answered faintly, "Yes," and again, "Yes, I think so." He handed me an old silver plate covered with lace, upon which were morsels of white bread, and I took a bit. Then he gave me a chalice of wine and bade me drink. I ate and drank. But the bread was dry and tasteless in my mouth, and the wine burned my tongue and I hated it. And I had to take off the white frock just as soon as we reached home. When it was all over it was rather disappointing.

Andrew, it seemed, could not live in entire peace even in America where there were no missionaries and, presumably, no heathen. The next memory I have of him is in an old rented house in a small college town in Virginia, we having gone there to be with my brother Edwin who was in the university. Andrew had no idea of settling down. He felt, since America was full of money, that he had better get what he could to carry on his work. So he deposited his family, or tried to do so. But there was some sort of difficulty about the house. It was rented from a stately old Virginia lady who lived in a huge columned affair on the hill above, and who, although she went regularly to church and dropped two coins into the plate on foreign mission Sundays, profoundly distrusted all missionaries when it came to personal dealings. Whether she had had previous unfortunate experiences, I do not know. But Andrew could brook arrogance from no one, having plenty of his own, and especially he could not endure it from females, whom he considered should be meek and yielding. It was a case of flint against flint, and a good many insults were given and taken.

It was not possible for a child fully to comprehend what was going on. One thing was clear. Andrew would not give her as much monthly rent as she wanted, and when she asked what guarantee she had for the year's rent, he replied with that furiously tranquil look of his, "The same guarantee, Madam, which I have—that the Lord provides for His own!" Evidently she was not fully reassured, in spite of being a Christian, for Andrew paused in the middle of a very favorite potato soup that night at supper to remark—as Carie put it, "out of a clear blue sky"—"That woman is a she-devil, that's what she is!"

"Why, Andrew!" Carie exclaimed.

We all waited for more, but Andrew had fallen placidly to his soup again, and there was no more. But whenever I saw Mrs. Estie riding by in her carriage, under a lace parasol, her ink-black coachman driving a pair of grey horses slowly down the tree-arched street, I looked at her hard. A she-devil! She sat very proud and erect, her white hair waved, her fine old profile conscious and haughty. She had once been a Southern belle and she had never got over it. But that disease is a curiously inverted one. It sickens almost to death any number of persons about her, but it remains robust and incurable in the woman who possesses it.

I have only one more memory of Andrew during that strange American year. He was almost always away, collecting money, but once he was at home and we were all going somewhere together to make a family call. I had, I remember, been dressed first, in a new frock of blue sprigged muslin. The skirt was smocked with blue silk upon a yoke, and the sleeves were short and puffed, and there was lace at the collarless neck. My long curls had been freshly spun about Carie's forefinger, and a blue bow sat on top of my head, and I swung my big hat. Thus arrayed, and feeling perfectly satisfied with myself, I stood at the steps into the street, waiting and spotless, when two small boys paused to stare. I pretended to pay no heed to them, of course, although I was acutely conscious of them. Indeed, I was a little sore from a recent experience with a detestable boy, the dunce of my third grade class, who had chosen to subject me to his adoration in spite of my furious and loud protestations of my hatred.

These two unknown and personable little boys, staring, were therefore in the nature of balm, although outwardly I appeared oblivious of them. At last one of them heaved a sigh and said to the other, "Ain't she pretty?"

But before he could answer I heard Andrew on the porch.

"Oh, pshaw!" he exclaimed. He had come out ready to go, and caught the little boy's remark.

"You go and find your mother!" he commanded me. And as I turned reluctantly, for I would not have dreamed of disobeying him, I saw the two little boys hastening up the street, pursued by his blue and baleful glare.

"Hm!" I heard him say loudly after them. And he stood there with a distasteful look upon his face, as though he smelled sin afar off.

Searching memory, we seem to be suddenly back in the square mission house again. After the crowded American year it was very still, very lonely. For us who were the children in Andrew's house, there were no white children to play with, and the days were long and filled with whatever we could find to put into them.

Certainly Andrew was not in them. For now began the most prosperous part of his missionary career. He came back with a good part of the money he had wanted and he found a strangely peaceful, an almost ominously peaceful, China. During the year something had happened. Instead of hostility he met everywhere a mask of courtesy and compliance. He could rent rooms anywhere he liked for chapels and schools, and people crowded into them. It is true that they seemed people of a new class, people with axes to grind, with difficulties to adjust, lawsuits, grievances, ambitions. Andrew found himself, as all white men did at that period, possessing a power of which he had been unconscious.

The explanation, of course, was the summary punishment given by the white men to the Chinese for the Boxer uprising. Word had gone all over the Chinese empire, that word flying like wind from mouth to mouth, more quick than written page or telegram today. White men, being strong and swift and fearful in retribution, came to be feared and hated and envied and admired and used. Every white man was a little king.

Andrew took it as God's triumph. He proceeded in great strides over that part of China which he considered his spiritual kingdom. With Ma the Christian to help and to advise and save him mistakes where he could be saved, he opened church after church, trained preachers to put in them who were responsible not only for their congregations but also for a certain amount of territory around them, and beside every church was a school. At one time Andrew had over two hundred churches and schools in his diocese. Twice a year he had a general assembly of all workers, and it was a sight to see the crowd who gathered to make report, to receive instructions and teaching. For Andrew never ceased to train and to develop and to teach those whom he had chosen to teach others. And Ma the

Christian was always at his elbow, dark and silent except for a whisper to which Andrew gave instant heed.

There was something curiously imperial about the whole thing, and none the less because it was an empire of the spirit, although Andrew was guileless to the core and had no such dreams. But dark Christians had such dreams, and that kingdom was not wholly of God. There were those in it who used the power of the name of the white man and the white man's religion to further their own ends. For in that time it was enough for a man to boast before a magistrate, "I belong to the white man's church, and I have his protection," for the magistrate to fall silent and give him his way without regard for justice.

But Andrew did not believe such things could be, and would not believe, though he were told. Andrew's children, looking back, remember that Carie told him a good many times and warned him often. She was nearer the common people than he could ever be. Women were not afraid of her and they gossiped and told tales, and she heard that the preacher Li was charging three silver dollars for every admission to the church and if anyone paid five, admission was sure, but if you tried to get in on the old confession of faith it was impossible. Or she heard that the older T'ing had three concubines secretly, and that the preacher Rao was an opium smoker. She repeated everything to Andrew, and he refused to believe anything.

It was a curious aspect of his nature that he was able to disbelieve anything he did not like to believe.

"If you would only try to see for yourself, Andrew," Carie would exclaim. "Don't let yourself be taken in!"

But Andrew would only answer, "It is the Lord's business, and his is the responsibility for these souls—not mine. I merely sow the good seed—he will separate the tares from the wheat."

It did not disturb him at all when a flagrant hypocrisy among them became open.

"Christ, too, had his Judas," he said, and was not troubled.

Carie was not the only one who battled with Andrew on this point. The other missionaries attacked him again and again and there were some who tried to discredit his whole work, feeling it was better to have only two converts and have them real, than Andrew's hundreds. But Andrew only laughed at them in his silent and dry fashion. He had a strange laugh, a wrinkling of his leathery face, a sudden shining in his eyes that did not in the least soften them, and one "Haw!" of sound. And with a touch of unaccustomed shrewdness he would say, "Polson and his precious pair of converts! Just as likely as not one's a hypocrite and that's fifty percent of his membership false! It's safer to have five hundred."

The missionaries made all sorts of checks and rules designed to curb Andrew's ways, but he was bound no more than Gulliver by the threads of the Lilliputians. He went his own way serenely, and they foamed and scolded and Andrew's children early were imbued with the feeling that the hands of their own kind were forever against their parents and therefore against them. Later, when they grew up, they were surprised to discover that these same people were good enough in their way, simple honest folk who were trying to do their duty as much as Andrew was. But between them and God were the mission officers and mission rules, while Andrew dealt only with God.

It fits here, perhaps, to tell Andrew's side of the war of the New Testament, which was the major entanglement and achievement of his life. Early in his career Andrew decided that the Chinese translation of the Bible was balderdash. There were all sorts of absurdities in it because, he said, the translators had not sufficiently understood Chinese idioms. Elijah's chariot, for instance, was translated "fire-wagon," a word later used for railway train, so that the passage led innocent heathen to believe that Elijah went to heaven on a railroad, and a good deal of geographical confusion resulted from this idea. Andrew decided, therefore, that as soon as he had time he would make a new translation straight from the Hebrew and Greek into Chinese. It was about this time that the missionaries themselves became convinced that they should have a new translation and chose a committee to make it, and Andrew's scholarly proficiency in the language being one thing at least which they appreciated, he was asked to be a member of the committee.

The scheme was simple. The New Testament was to be the first portion translated, and its chapters were divided among the committee in equal shares. Each man was supposed to work on his share at home with an approved Chinese scholar to help him, and in the summer they were to meet at a chosen spot to compare, criticize and confer upon each other's work.

It was to Andrew a work of the most sacred sort. With Ma as his aide, he pored at night over his assignment, all through one winter and spring. Early in July he and Ma went north to the meeting place. There was a certain solemnity about the departure. Carie had been at great pains to furbish up his clothes and by dint of much talk and some flattery she had persuaded him to get a new white suit. Her saint should be as personable as any of them.

He was to be away eight weeks. We settled down to the long hot summer with a certain sense of freedom. With Andrew gone leisure descended upon the house like coolness over heat. We all had things we wanted to do. Carie was going to teach me how to sing alto that summer, and she had saved up a little secret hoard out of the housekeeping money and had bought from Shanghai four new books that we were going to read aloud—two of them novels for a treat. And we were going to make new curtains for the living room. And Carie was going to have the umbrella tree cut out of the garden. Trees were a continual argument between Andrew and Carie. Carie loved sunshine, but in the warm heat of the Yangtse Valley the trees grew huge and weedy and shaded the house and made the mildew grow overnight like frost upon shoes and garments and the straw matting. But Andrew never wanted any tree cut down at all. The umbrella tree had been a particular bone between them. He would not hear of its being cut, although its huge fan-like leaves flapped all over one corner of the porch, and the garden snakes loved to creep around its wet branches. Carie abhorred the tree and her too quick imagination imbued it with a sinister influence. She had said months before to us, "The minute Andrew is out of the house this summer I'm going to have that tree cut down. He makes a fuss for it, but I don't believe he'll notice it if it's gone."

And Andrew was scarcely out of the compound gate before she had the gardener chopping at it. She stood triumphantly to see it fall. It fell with a groan and instantly a great beam of sunlight shot into the shadows of the porch.

"There!" Carie said. "I can breathe again!"

It was well she did not delay, for in less than two weeks Andrew was back. He had told us nothing, for his letters were always noncommittal. "The flies in Chefoo are fearful," he had written. "It is an Egyptian plague and the mosquitoes are worse." He made a few complaints about his fellow workers. "Barton is lazy. He does not begin work before eight o'clock of mornings. It's his English morning tea habits and too big a breakfast, I tell him." But later there had been other more severe complaints of the English missionary. Andrew wrote in every letter, "Barton wants everything his own way." Carie, reading that, laughed and said, "There isn't another like him there, is there?" She wrote him, counseling patience, forbearance, the possibility that eight might be more right than one, and the majority should decide. But when did majority mean anything to Andrew, who was so used to being the minority of one? "Barton is insufferable," he wrote.

"I'm afraid Andrew isn't going to make it," said Carie regretfully.

It was the day after that he appeared, Mr. Ma darkly silent behind him. Andrew had on his new white suit, which he had forgotten to wear before, but had remembered when he thought of seeing Carie. He looked splendid and triumphant and very happy to be home. He was unusually jovial all evening, although we could not make out much of what the trouble had been, except that Andrew had wholly approved of no one's translation except his own. In fairness to him it must be said that this seemed to be a fairly unanimous state of mind among the committee. But Barton had been the worst.

"The fellow isn't even educated," Andrew said, eating his supper with a vast relish. "He quit school at sixteen and went into a draper's shop in London—he doesn't know a word of Hebrew and Greek."

"Maybe he knows Chinese," Carie said. She was always somewhat inclined to take the other side against Andrew.

"Pshaw!" said Andrew. "I have no confidence in him."

"What are you going to do now?" we asked.

"Make the translation myself," he replied.

"So you will know it's right?" asked Carie, laughing.

But Andrew looked at her with surprise and gravity.

"Exactly," he replied.

As for the umbrella tree, Carie was right. He never noticed it was gone, although two years later, when Carie in a mischievous mood told him of it, he instantly declared he had missed something all along, and had not known what it was. And he was so positive that we did not dare to laugh until he had left the room.

So in that manner began the work which to Andrew's children took on, as the years passed, the aspect of a giant inexorable force which swallowed their toys, their few pleasures, their small desires, into its being and left them very little for their own. But that does not matter in this tale. For to Andrew it was excitement, creation, fulfillment. And he had the need to create, unrealized until now.

More and more he put the work of superintending the churches and schools into the hands of the Christian Ma, and more and more he immersed himself in Greek roots, in Pauline theology, in Chinese idioms. He withdrew yet further from the world, spending days and nights in his inviolable study. We could hear the strange music of Greek as he read aloud the text, and the chanting intonations of the Chinese. Slowly, very slowly, the heap of pages in Greek, interlined with Chinese written in his large script, grew upon the table under the paperweight which was a Buddha that one of his converts had once worshipped, renounced, and given to him, and which now stood there ironically holding together the Christian scriptures.

His fellow missionaries objected vigorously to this use of Andrew's time. Nobody, they said, had given him permission to translate the New Testament alone.

"Nobody except God!" said Andrew, and he looked as high and as cold as an alp.

Most of these wars and skirmishes between Andrew and his fellow missionaries took place, not from day to day, but at an annual gathering known as "mission-meeting," where all the missionaries and their wives came together to give report and to discuss rules and make laws and policies. Not that the wives had anything, presumably, to do with it. The mission of the church in which

Andrew had been bred and now worked was and still is made up of a group of Americans from the South, who present a mixture of human qualities of the most curious and fascinating sort. To this day they maintain an incredible narrowness of creed which accepts in entirety the miracles of virgin birth, water changed into wine, the dead raised to life, and the second appearance, hourly expected, of Christ. Their judgment upon those who do not or cannot so believe is inhumanly cruel—such persons simply do not exist for them—no friendship is possible, no acquaintance desired. But within their own group of sympathizers they are friendly and kind enough, endlessly helpful in illness or need. Religion in their case, as in so many another, has hardened their hearts and made it impossible for them to see, except through the dark glass of their own creed, what life is or ought to be.

One of the more amusing aspects of their creed was the wholehearted adoption of St. Paul's contempt of women. In that little band of missionaries no woman ever raised her voice before men, either to pray or to speak in meeting. In their meetings the women knelt mutely before the men, who knelt before God and alone could speak to him. And Andrew was one of them. Once at a prayer meeting an English woman of another faith in all innocence prayed aloud when, according to the custom, the meeting was thrown open for prayer. Three out of the five men present rose and stalked out. I opened my eyes to see how Andrew was bearing it. He was restive upon his knees, but Carie was kneeling beside him, her eyes wide open, fixed upon him, daring him to move. Andrew would not look at Carie and he did not go out, but he was doing what no one had ever seen him do before—his eyes were wide open and he was staring out of the window. As far as he was concerned, there was no praying going on.

The annual mission meeting was, therefore, as good as a circus. For the wives of these early missionaries were no weaklings. They were pioneers as much as their men were, and if they could not speak in public they made up for it by a great deal of private speaking. There was Mrs. Houston, for instance, from Georgia. Everybody knew the story about her. When Mr. Houston came to marry her on their way to China, he grew nervous as the train approached the town where she lived and he went straight on to the coast and took sail, without stopping for the wedding at all, although the bride was dressed and waiting and all the guests were in the church. But Jenny Houston was not in the least daunted. She packed up her wedding finery and came straight after him in Shanghai and married him and made him a strong, able, domineering wife, who in a voice, full of Southern softness and drawl, commanded him altogether for his own good.

And there was Sallie Gant, so much better a preacher than gentle little Lem Gant, her husband—Sallie who proclaimed loudly her complete obedience to the Pauline creed and bowed her handsome blonde head to that yoke. And yet no one needed to do more than see the two together to know that Sallie had Lem's gentle soul between her thumb and forefinger and that she pinched it cruelly.

For of course the inevitable result of this religious subjection of women was to breed in them an irrepressible independence and desire for self-expression, born of their innate and unconscious sense of injury and injustice. All subject people so suffer. If men were wise they would give women complete freedom and their rebellions would dissipate into mildness and uncertainty.

But in those repressed, strong, vigorous missionary women the blood ran high. Their very faces were stormy and hewn into lines of determination and grimness, with more often than not a touch of humor. There was a good deal of pathos about them, too, particularly among those not yet quite old, who still longed for a little pleasure or were interested in a new dress or what "the styles" were at home. If one were to choose between the men and the women, the women would have won for the look of strong patience in their eyes and for the stubbornness upon their lips. And in mission meeting, though only the men could rise and speak before the assembly, beside every man sat his woman, her hand ready to grasp his coat tails. How many times I have seen a man leap to his feet, his grizzled beard working, his eyes flashing, and open his mouth to speak, only to sit abruptly, subdued by a strong downward pull upon his coat tails! There would be a vigorous whispered conference between man and woman. Sometimes he was as stubborn as she, and if he could not say what he wanted, he would say nothing. But more often he stood up again after a few moments, the fire gone from his eyes, and clearing his throat, he would begin to speak, and his voice came out as mild as a summer wind. They all knitted, those women, while their men gave reports and passed laws of the church and made prayers. Their strong hard fingers flew while they had to remain mute. Into those stitches went what curbed desires and stubborn wills and plans! They would have burst, I think, without that vent.

But there were some women who were not married and had no men to speak for them. These did full work in the mission and then they wrote out the report each year of what they had done and asked some man to read it for them, and sat silent while men voted what money they should be given and what they should do with it. There was little Dr. Greene, for instance, who ran a big hospital for women and children and had a school for nurses besides, and was one of the most extraordinary women who ever lived. Florence Nightingale's life was a mild story compared to Dr. Greene's lonely hourly struggle in that far interior city of China. She was very beloved and the sick came to her from far and near, for they trusted her. Yet every year she gave the written report of her thousands of cases, her incredible, terrific operations, her huge numbers of lives saved, to some man who read it aloud to other men and then they voted what she could and could not do. It is true she sat peacefully smiling, not knitting, just resting for once, and when they had decided for her, she went back again and did exactly as she pleased. But I remember her best thus: I as a child was once in the courtyard of her hospital and a poor slave girl was brought in dying of opium which she had swallowed. Dr. Greene, hearing of her extremity, rushed into the courtyard, but it was too late—the poor thing died at that instant.

I had seen plenty of dead people, even at that age, but this was my first sight of a soul passing out of a body. And the girl was so pretty—so pretty! I could not keep from crying and I begged Dr. Greene, "She won't go to hell, will she? God wouldn't send her to hell, would he?"

Dr. Greene's gentle pale face moved a little, and she sighed, "I don't know, my child—I don't know. It doesn't bear thinking about." And she stroked the girl's fading, cooling hand.

It was a heresy, of course. It would never have done to say such a thing in the presence of the saints. Not to know! It was a sin not to know.

And yet these stormy, human Christian saints, as full of their original sin as any people could be, with none of the tempered grace of the civilized heathen whom they were trying to convert, could at the appointed hour lay aside their differences and their furies, and together break the bread and drink the wine of communion, and then a strange strong peace filled the house in which they sat. It was the peace of complete belief in that which they lived, the absolute certainty of their minds, the total surrender of their souls to that to which they had committed themselves. It made no difference whether, absolutely speaking, they were right or wrong. They came, believing they brought salvation and happiness to all who accepted their creed. And in a sense they were right. All who could believe as they believed were saved from the doubt and distrust and the unhappiness bred of a mind uncertain of its own being. But none were as happy as they were themselves, for none were so blind in their sureness. Their hearts were empty and swept, the light in their minds extinguished. No question was allowed to enter them. One of them once roared at me, discovering in my trembling hands Darwin's *Origin of Species,* "I would no more think of reading a book against my belief or talking with an unbeliever except to preach to him, than I would of taking poison into my body." Yes, they built their own citadel, and the walls were high as heaven, and there was only one small gate by which to enter. But if there was war within, there was also peace.

Andrew always came out of the mission meetings greatly whetted and refreshed by the conflict and by the communion. He was one of perhaps three men in the group of two score or more who paid no attention to any pull on his coat tails. Sometimes Carie, driven to speak by intense disagreement, would make her whispering at his ear, but I never knew him to be in the least affected by it—that is, not in the way she hoped. "Oh, pshaw!" he would say aloud, and get up in his seemingly mild fashion and say exactly what he had been going to say anyway. The knowledge of impotence was bitter in Carie. "Your father is stubborn as a mule," she once said passionately, and then added furiously, "and he's right a good deal of the time, which doesn't make things any easier!" However Carie might complain privately about Andrew, publicly she always upheld him.

Once, in a romantic adolescent moment, dreaming over Tennyson's *Princess,* I looked up to ask her, "Mother, were you and Father ever in love?"

She was sewing at some everyday garment, and for a moment I could not fathom her sudden look at me. It was—was it pain, shock—what was it? But it was not surprised enough for pain or shock. It was as though I had opened a secret, unconsciously. Then the look closed.

"Your father and I have both been very busy people," she said, her voice practical and a little brisk. "We have thought of our duty rather than how we felt." She turned a hem quickly and went on sewing.

But Andrew was not to be moved by wifely counsel or by love. It was about this time that he developed a new war. There was, of course, always the war of the New Testament. Each year in mission meeting he reported how many more chapters were done, and listened benignly while the others voted he was not to go on with it and that no money was to be given him for it. But the new war had to do with the establishment of a center for training Chinese clergy, a theological seminary, in short.

It was an enterprise far too large for any one group to begin and maintain, but several denominations had decided to subscribe to it, and Andrew's denomination was contemplating the matter. From the first Andrew was eager for it. To found a stable seat of training for the leaders of the Chinese church—his mind leaped ahead, planning. And he had risen to his feet at once to speak for it.

So was begun that long war which was continued year after year. For Andrew and a few others had overpersuaded, by their fiery tongues, the more conservative majority. It soon appeared that the union would never work. There were the Methodists and their bishops concerning whom Andrew remarked drily, "They are perfectly willing to unite with everybody provided everybody joins the Methodists." And the Baptists who insisted that the budding Chinese clergy must be taught the essential doctrine of immersion, and the Episcopalians—but then, no one expected the Episcopalians to join anything. And most dreadful of all were the sects which were tinged with modernism. It soon became evident that union with other denominations was impossible, and the war was on. But year after year at mission meeting, Andrew, son of generations of grim Presbyterian fathers, Calvinist, predestinarian, believer in the second coming of Christ, fought the battle for union.

"Not for modernism," he would proclaim when he was accused. "Never! But the only way to change a thing is to stay in it and change it from within. You can never accomplish anything by pulling out and going off by yourself!"

It was a long losing war, continued over twenty years. I say losing, because his denomination pulled away at last from the union—they came, every man and woman of them, from seceding Southern blood. But Andrew never gave up. He flouted them all by giving the last years of his life to the union from which the majority had long since voted to withdraw. But then, as I said, a majority vote meant nothing to Andrew. He spent all his life being a ruling minority of one.

In these eight triumphant years after the Boxer Rebellion Andrew saw his work established over a wide territory. His lists of converts were well up into hundreds each year. His New Testament translation he was publishing book by book as he finished it, and the four Gospels he put into one early volume. Again he was heaped with criticism—it was, they said, too "common" in its style.

For again Andrew was too forward for his times. He had already realized that one strong reason for ignorance and illiteracy in China was that the language of books and the language of the people were entirely different. It was a situation paralleled in ancient England, where almost all literature was in Latin, of which the common man knew nothing. Andrew, therefore, in deciding to use a simple vernacular style in his translation of the Greek New Testament, was revolutionary in the extreme, antedating by a score of years those later Chinese revolutionaries who brought about what was called the Chinese Renaissance, on exactly the same principle that Andrew had seen so clearly. But they were too patriotic ever to recognize as forerunner a white man and a Christian.

Andrew had chosen, then, to use not the classical Chinese beloved of old scholars but the strong vernacular mandarin of the people. He could not, it is true, make it too vernacular, because of his own purist instincts, but he chose a clear, somewhat compressed, plain style, without allusion or furbishing, corresponding somewhat to the Moffatt edition of the English Bible. The few old Chinese scholars who were converts complained that the vernacular had no literary value, and that Andrew had made a book fit only for the common people. Andrew, himself a scholar, smiled his wry independent smile.

"Exactly!" he said. "Now when a common man learns to read a little he can make something out of Christ's teaching."

And he went on translating and polishing each book as he finished it, paying for it all by incredible pinchings and scrapings and even begging. He was not in the least proud about begging for money to carry on his work. He scattered his little books everywhere he went. But he would never give them away, having observed that any bits of valueless paper procurable were at once made into shoe soles by the indefatigable Chinese wives. So he made everybody pay a penny or two for salvation. But he paid more than any of them.

All these years Andrew's children were growing up in his house. In after years, after he had been old and was dead, they looked at each other trying to remember him, but they could not. They remembered him in certain moments of vivid action, but there was no continuity to their memories. The days went on without him in the peaceful busy round of the house. He came home at certain times and nothing seemed quite natural until he was gone again. They tiptoed about, because he was tired, they fetched his slippers and books, they gave up Carie to him, and wandered a little desolately on the fringe of rather stormy talk about "the Work," or about the newly come missionary. "A good man, but not overly bright," Andrew summed him up at the dinner table.

These visits of Andrew's to his home were not perhaps entirely fair to him, for Carie was too soft-hearted to whip any of her children, and yet she had been reared in the belief that to spare the rod was to spoil the child. So major punishments were reserved for Andrew's coming. He did not waste much time over causes. After all, there were only two or three things a child could do which in Carie's opinion merited whipping and chief of them was a lie. And he always took Carie's word.

Andrew, in his study, would look up from his book at a small liar, standing trembling before him. "Go out and cut me a switch," he would say with ominous mildness. When it was brought in, he examined it for size and pliability. It need not be large, but it must not be small.

"Down with your things!" he said, if he were satisfied. He turned in his swivel chair. "Stand still!" he commanded.

We never thought of disobeying him, or even of roaring unduly, although with Carie and her wavering punishments we bellowed shamelessly in the full knowledge of her soft heart. But once the most naughty of Andrew's children bent the switch secretly in a dozen places and presented it thus, apparently whole but really shorn of its strength. Andrew laid it upon the small thigh where it fell harmlessly. He saw instantly that he had been deceived. "Oh, pshaw!" he exclaimed. A glint of steely humor came into his eyes, but he rose and went out and cut a beautiful switch from a willow tree and snipped off the twigs and smoothed it down to extremest efficiency.

But wait! There were a few times—was it perhaps Christmas Eve or a birthday?—when Andrew played crokinole with us. We do not remember any other games with him. Carie played checkers and taught us chess, which she loved, and advised Authors for our education. But one year the Montgomery Ward boxes held a crokinole board, and there were evenings when Andrew played. He enjoyed it immensely, taking an unexpected pleasure in it, and forgetting everything else for the moment. He had an extraordinarily long strong forefinger and great accuracy of aim, and he knocked the little round wooden pieces with terrific force into the net bags where they were supposed to go. We all crouched a little and held our breaths, because if they hit a small peg in the middle of the board they bounced and struck like a shot. One small daughter of his went with a sore spot on her little breast bone for days.

And wait again! There were certain other evenings when prayers with the servants being over, he read aloud to us all and to Carie while she sewed. It was always the *Century Magazine,* to which he subscribed regularly for many years, and each year sent to Shanghai to be bound. There were years of them in a row on the bottom shelf in his study, and one after the other of his children in their time stole in and surreptitiously slipped out a volume and spread out the others to cover the space. For they wanted the books for the stories in them and Andrew did not approve of "story books." Only once did he read aloud a novel and he was inveigled into it by seeing the first few pages inadvertently. He had picked the book up to forbid it, and glancing at it had broken into his "haw" of laughter at a sentence he saw. The book was *The Casting Away of Mrs. Lecks and Mrs. Aleshine.* He kept on turning over the leaves and we held our breaths again. He put it down and said nothing. But after supper he took it up.

"I suppose you'd like this," he said to Carie and began to read it aloud. We all sat and listened and laughed, and none of us laughed as much as Andrew. His eyes would run ahead and begin to shine and his voice choked and his face turned red. He tried to go on, but it was too funny for him. He laid the book down to laugh and to gasp over and over, "Oh, pshaw—oh, pshaw!"

It was a sad day when it was over. We had never had such a good time before. I have never seen the book again, but it remains to me the funniest book in the world. Not even Mark Twain was quite so funny. Carie thought Mark Twain a little coarse and Andrew found his humor marred by certain irreligious tendencies. But Mrs. Lecks and Mrs. Aleshine! They were two absurd and delightful old women, and Andrew could laugh at them with no sense of sin. Remembering, one day, it made us wonder what manner of man Andrew might have been with that strong wry sense of humor—what manner of man he might have been, that is, if God had not caught his soul and Calvin had not held fast his heart!

IX

THAT those successful years were happy ones I know from Andrew's own record. "It seemed that before I knew it eight years were gone and it was again time for furlough." The early term of service had been ten years; now it was shortened to eight—an unnecessarily short time, Andrew felt. For why should a man need a rest from work which his soul delighted to do? He would have taken no furlough except that a daughter was ready to be sent back to college, and Carie wanted to go with her. America was strange and different now, and the child was used to nothing but these quiet Chinese villages and hills. Besides, there were the kinfolk. So grudgingly Andrew gave up the year, consoling himself with the hope of getting money for his work and of working on his translation.

To those children of his who accompanied him that was a memorable journey. For Carie suddenly decided that she could not again cross the Pacific which made her desperately ill, that the children ought to see Europe, that she wanted to see Russia, and that they would therefore all go up the Yangtse River to Hankow and take train for the north and thence to Russia and Siberia by train to Germany. It was a stupendous plan, for we always remembered that Andrew was no executive when it came to the matter of tickets. He could direct the efforts of hundreds of churches and schools and thousands of souls, but the intricacies of ticket buying confused him. The whole journey was a series of major and minor catastrophes. His children remember less of Russia than they do of Andrew, cooped up in a small railway compartment with nowhere to put his long legs all day. He who needed space and privacy was reduced to nothing of either.

There was not even a lavatory, and we were compelled to do all our washing in turn out of a small enamelled basin we had brought along, and water was very scarce and to be had only at stations and then by rushing out with a can and buying it.

There was one dreadful morning when the smallest child forgot to empty the basin after she had used it, and Andrew, always absent-minded and now in deepest gloom over his situation, sat down in it and ruined his only pair of trousers. He had not recovered from this when he found a cup half full of water, and wanting to use the cup, he threw the contents out of the window. He was too nearsighted to see that the glass was up, and the water flew back at him, wetting his front very thoroughly. Carie laughed. It was too much. He sat down. "There is nothing to laugh at," he said severely, and for the rest of the day he stared gloomily at the flat Russian landscape and muttered over and over, "I don't see anything to this country—there's nothing to make a fuss over, here!" The hearty Russian fashion of kissing appalled him. He watched the bearded dirty peasants greet each other with loud kisses and shuddered. This was worse than a heathen country, he said.

Later, he was to grow more appalled. When we stopped at various places for a few days he wandered inevitably to the churches, and stood there by the hour, watching the hordes of people come in, poor and ragged and miserable, most of them, but a few of them rich too, and poor and rich all bending to kiss the relics of cloth or bone or skin left from some dead saint. Strangely, he felt no pity or responsibility for these souls. "They have the Bible," he said. "They could get at the truth if they would. But it's an easy way—to live in sin and go and gabble to a priest and kiss a bone and call it salvation!"

So we were all glad when we got Andrew into Germany, and yet the very first day in Berlin we saw a sight we had never yet seen—Andrew so incensed that he offered to fight a cabman! The fellow was a huge, burly, heavy German and he shook his fist under Andrew's nose in the railway station in the presence of innumerable people because he considered his tip inadequate, whereupon Andrew, who felt tips were of the devil anyhow, doubled up his fists and pushed them into the fellow's fat jaw. We were so amazed we could not believe this was our Andrew. Carie screamed and held his arm and fumbled in her own bag for coins to placate the Teuton, and at last roaring throaty oaths, he went his way, and we led Andrew hastily to a hotel, taking care to hire the meekest looking porter in sight to transport our bags. Andrew went with us, looking more ungodly than we would have believed possible, giving as he went his opinion of the white race, which for the moment was even lower than usual. Indeed, I believe this incident more than anything else was responsible for Andrew's strong stand against the Germans in the World War, and his complete readiness to believe all atrocity stories.

"That fellow!" he would mutter for years after, "the Germans are capable of anything!"—this in spite of his own early German ancestry and an innocent pride he always took in his proficiency in the German language.

How Andrew looked in America a certain daughter of his will always remember. She sat, a timid freshman among other freshmen in a college chapel, waiting in some anxiety. For Andrew had been asked to lead vespers, and among the few friends she had eagerly made, the first friends of her own race she had ever had, she was anxious that all impressions be of the best. She looked at Andrew with some misgiving as he came in, tranquil as ever, behind the president. No man could move with greater dignity than he before a service he was to give. Everybody looked at him and his daughter saw him with new detachment, a very tall, slightly stooped figure, the noble head carried with native pride, his big profile pointed straight ahead. But then she only saw that his frock coat was the same old coat, rusty and given a little at the seams and of an obsolete cut, and well she knew the scene there had been before he put it on.

Carie said, "Andrew, you're not going to preach at the college in that old grey suit!"

"Old! It's not old—it's a good suit—good enough for a preacher."

"Andrew!" Carie's dark eyes went on speaking, fixed upon him. He looked away from her doggedly.

"A preacher oughtn't to be all dressed up," he muttered.

Her eyes, pinning him, went on speaking.

He went on, restlessly, "I tell you I hate that old long-tailed coat! The armholes are tight."

"I've been wanting you to get a new one for years." Carie's voice was dangerously mild.

"What for?" Andrew demanded. "It's perfectly good!"

"Then why won't you wear it?"

"Oh, pshaw!" he said, and got up, beaten.

There was a whisper beside his daughter in the chapel. A girlish voice said in a soft, innocent, Southern drawl, "He looks as though he'd be right long-winded!"

There was a bitter moment and then Andrew's daughter said, her lips dry, "He's my father."

There was a shock of silence. "Oh, I *am* sorry!" the pretty voice said.

"It doesn't matter," said Andrew's daughter sternly. "He *is* long-winded!" and sat there suffering, while Andrew preached on and on.

For she never knew what to do with him. He fitted into no niche as a father. Great missionary he was, intrepid soul, but there was no fatherhood in him. He had to be viewed, to be considered, not as a father but as a man. His children were merely accidents which had befallen him. Else how explain that amazing incident when having discovered to his horror the minimum cost of a college education, he decided he would not rob the New Testament and so wrote to a certain rich man of his acquaintance to ask if he did not want to educate an incipient missionary? Carie, opening in his absence the polite, amazed refusal, was quite out of her mind with outraged pride and could not keep it to herself. That daughter of hers, hearing, was struck to the heart. She felt somehow that she had been sold into slavery. The ugly college sitting-room where she and Carie sat is forever imprinted upon her mind. From outside came the voices of girls, American girls, born free of the bondage which all unconsciously Andrew had laid upon his children. Not one of them knew what it was to be always nothing in comparison to a cause, to a work, to a creed.

"He needn't bother about me," she said, strangling with

pride and hurt. "I can look out for myself. I'll leave college this very day and go and get a job at the ten cent store. I can look after myself. He doesn't even need to feed me."

"Don't—don't take it so!" Carie begged her. Tears were in her eyes. "I oughtn't to have told you. He didn't mean anything—you've got to understand that he isn't like other men. He's—he's like somebody in a dream!"

Yes, that was it. Andrew was somebody in a dream, a soul possessed, to whom life and the human heart had no importance. He never lived on earth. She knew what Carie meant. She did not blame Andrew, not really—but she felt herself fatherless. In after years she grew closer to him, as close as any human could, and came to understand and value him, to know why he was as he was, both great and small. But all that later knowledge cannot quite wipe away the bereavement of that hour. For Andrew's children were bereaved in what they never had, in what he could not give them, because he had given everything in him to God.

Andrew came back to find again a new China. During all those years of too great peace, too easy triumph of God's will, something had been happening. It was a deep rebellion, a revolution brewing upward from the South, taking that easiest way of all revolutions, of antagonism to the foreigner and an outburst of nationalism. Andrew and Carie and their youngest child were scarcely back in the square mission bungalow when the false peace of eleven years exploded, and Sun Yat-sen and his followers overthrew the old empire.

It is another story, often told and belonging now to history, and other events have robbed it of much meaning. But Andrew at the time viewed it with enthusiasm. He was so weary of the corruption of Chinese officials with whom he had often to deal that he would have welcomed any force, even to an earthquake and their being swallowed up. So when old careless opium-smoking viceroys and mandarins and magistrates began to escape into hiding, he took open part with the revolutionists. Especially was he happy at the passing of the Empress Dowager. He could see no drama or beauty in that splendid old figure. To him she was that most horrible and unnatural of all creations, a woman ruler. He did not even hold Queen Elizabeth in honor. Indeed, his estimation was low of any nation willing to set a woman to rule. "Jezebel," he called the Empress Dowager, and would recount with relish the end of that queen, when having been thrown from her high tower she was devoured by dogs. There was that in Andrew which could have stood by gladly and watched it as a just retribution. Born a generation earlier, he would have burned witches. There was a deep unconscious sex antagonism in him, rooted in no one knows what childhood experiences and fostered, sad to say, by the presence of Carie, that flashing quick mind which he could never comprehend, but against which he struggled to maintain himself. For he could not bear better than another man a woman more clever than himself. Besides, St. Paul justified him.

He allied himself, therefore, with the young men's revolution. For it was a young men's revolution and Andrew was always drawn to young men. He gloried in every step they took—even in their ruthless new laws that cut off queues by force. Andrew liked ruthlessness. A thing was always either right or wrong, and if it was right, it was right to enforce it.

It was somewhat dismaying to discover that in spite of Sun Yat-sen's being a Christian, there was a strong anti-Christian feeling in the revolution. But Andrew had complete faith in the triumph of God. "Tares in the wheat," he said. "God will uproot them and cast them into the fire."

So he began again his long journeys by horseback and by boat. Ma the Christian had held the churches together wonderfully well, working with that dark burning eagerness which was so compelling that it made men uncomfortable, not sure whether it was good or evil. He had been so much with Andrew and he so loved him that he had unaware taken for his own many of Andrew's gestures and tricks of speaking and preaching. If one shut one's eyes and only listened, it would have been hard to tell which of them was preaching or praying.

But Ma was not a revolutionist. He had not Andrew's optimism and guileless faith in men who said their purpose was good. He kept silent publicly, but in many ways he restrained Andrew.

"Let us wait twenty years and see," he kept saying to him, "twenty years for a test." When the years had passed and most of the self-denying ardent revolutionists were long established in power and had reverted to all the old official corruption and to not a few tricks from the West besides, he was quietly complacent. "No governor is good," he said. "A good governor has never been heard of, in the past or now."

But Andrew could not believe ill of young men. And he welcomed every change—indeed, he had a childlike love of the new, always thinking it must be better than what was old. Not until he was set upon and stoned in a certain city by young revolutionists, and driven out because he preached a foreign religion and was a citizen of an imperialistic foreign power, did he even concede the presence of tares. Imperialism! It was the first time he had heard that word, but he was to hear it often in the years to come. He never had any idea what it meant. "It's one of those words people use," he used to say in his own imperial fashion, and there was an end of it.

But his work proceeded with increasing difficulty. He

had long since so enlarged his territory that the white horse, which had replaced his donkey, was growing old, and was not enough. The newly running train to Shanghai reached a part of his field, but there was a large area which could be reached only by boat. For years Andrew had waged battles with junk men in the process of hiring a small junk to take him along the interior canals of the country.

The boatmen of China are undoubtedly and universally of the breed of pirates. There is not one who has not a pirate's heart born in him. Time and again Andrew would be delayed in setting forth on a tour because the boat captain was demanding more money than he had agreed upon. So the idea came to Andrew to buy his own boat, and he happened to have a sum of money for it. A man in America had given it to him to build a chapel in memory of his dead wife, but Andrew decided it would be more useful to God to buy a boat with the money. It did not occur to him that the donor might not want a boat in memory of his wife. And according to his custom, Andrew, having thought of a good thing, proceeded instantly to its completion. Only when the boat was built and finished did he write to the man and tell him that there was a boat instead of a chapel.

Andrew did not at all anticipate the outcome. The man was filled with fury. It seemed his wife was always seasick and particularly hated boats. He refused the boat and demanded the return of the money at once.

Andrew was amazed at such lack of reason. He folded the man's letter and remarked in a tone of complete and calm righteousness, "How can he ask for the money back when he knows it is spent? Besides, I told him very clearly that a boat would be more useful now to me than a chapel." With infinite dignity he added, "I shall pay no attention to him." It was perhaps his most frequently repeated phrase in a disagreement.

But the man was a rich man, accustomed to having his own way, and he considered Andrew as a little higher than a menial, but not much. Missionaries! What were they? Servants of the church, and he practically owned the church, because he gave it so much money. He complained furiously to Andrew's mission board, who wrote to Andrew sternly. This board, it happened, was the one organization Andrew heeded somewhat, because it could deprive him of all funds, salary as well as work funds, and he never distinguished clearly between the two. He used money as long as it was there, chiefly for his work. Even Carie could not touch it. He did not believe in women having check books, and the idea of a joint bank account filled him with horror.

"Why, you might take out money, and I wouldn't know where I was!" he exclaimed once in consternation when she suggested a check book of her own.

"I never know where I am!" Carie retorted. "I have to feed and clothe you and the children and I never know what there is to count on."

It was a crisis in a long war between them, waged through their whole life. Andrew never thought food and clothes ought to cost anything. Anyway, the Work came first. Carie made miracles out of pennies, but he never knew it. She said once with a twinkle and a sigh, "Andrew ought to have married that widow in the Bible who had a bottomless cruse of oil and a flour bin that was never empty. Ever since he heard of her nothing I can do satisfies him!"

But he was harder on himself than on anyone else, and none ate more frugally or clothed himself more poorly than he, for God's sake. Nevertheless, there was that war between them, and it went on for forty years, when suddenly, for no apparent reason, Andrew gave up one day and handed her a check book to a joint account. Carie by that time was past the need of it. The children were grown and her great desires were over. Nevertheless, for victory's sake she took it and under direction made out a check or two and then put the book away. But it was a comfort to her. She could draw a check if she wanted to, at last.

To be confronted, then, by his mission board with a demand that he account for a thousand dollars given for a chapel and spent on a boat was somewhat terrifying even to Andrew, and catastrophe to Carie. She reproached him, seeing her children with nothing, and in a foreign country where the people were increasingly unfriendly.

"If you wouldn't be so headstrong!" she said mournfully, and quite hopelessly. Andrew not headstrong would not be Andrew.

But any such reproach was always strength to Andrew's purpose. "I know what I'm doing," he said severely.

Unfortunately for its own authority, the board member who wrote the letter was foolish enough to add, thinking it would be a whip over Andrew, "Mr. Shipley is one of our wealthiest donors and it is most unwise to offend him in any way."

A glitter of ice shone in Andrew's eyes as he read this. So he was to obey a man merely because he was rich! A rich man could very hardly enter the Kingdom of Heaven, and yet he, Andrew, was to obey him before God! He sat down at once in the freshness of his scorn and wrath, and wrote what his children called one of his God-almighty letters, inquiring of the board in simple, brief phrases what they meant by bowing their heads to Mammon and how they thought themselves worthy of their positions as directors of God's work? As for him, he would not listen to any rich man or to them, but only to God. The boat was built and he would use it.

He never again heard anything on the subject from either the rich man or the board, and he used the boat happily and in triumph for many years until he grew too old to make his journeys any more.

After the first success of the revolution was over it came to be apparent that the changes it had brought about were not fundamental. Sun Yat-sen, living so many years abroad as to have become a foreigner in his own country, made a profound mistake in the object of his revolution. Observing Western countries, he decided that a good central government could make all the changes he longed for in China, and that the first and most important step was to change the form of that government, and this he did, and it remains the chief thing he did do. For what he did not understand was that central government in China is not important as it is in many other countries, and never has been. The life of the people, their lives and rules of life, have proceeded not from central government but from themselves and out of their family and group life. To overthrow a central government and change its form was not of deep importance to the people. The Chinese people have not, as has England or the United States or France, created slowly, by one means and another step by step through centuries, their own form of central government. Such government in China has been primarily by conquerors, either native war lords or foreign ones, who established a sort of suzerainty. The people were not ruled by them in the sense that other governments rule by force or laws made and obeyed. The life of the people went on, therefore, in the same old ways fundamentally, because the real and local government was not changed.

And the foreign powers made haste to present claims and protect treaties and the lives of their citizens. The weak new revolutionary government, inexperienced and easily alarmed, did not dare to create enmity so soon. Within a very few years Andrew was able to proceed as boldly and safely as ever, preaching wherever he would, and because he was a foreigner he was free to do as he liked. Again his work prospered.

It never occurred to any of us that Andrew could ever grow old. His body had always been the same, lean as a pine, his skin weathered to a dark bronze red. He never added a pound to his weight, and his waist stayed as slim as it had ever been in his youth. There never was, in fact, a saint who had the flesh so subdued as he. Wherever he was, in whatever inconvenience of circumstance, his regimen remained immovably the same—a cold bath at rising, and he rose invariably at half-past five; from six to seven he spent in prayer and meditation; at seven he breakfasted, invariably the same breakfast, and it always included a dish of porridge made from native wheat washed and sun dried and ground in a little stone hand mill. Work began immediately after breakfast and continued until noon, when he dined, to work again until five o'clock, when he walked for an hour before his supper. In the evening he preached at some chapel, or if he were free, he read and was in bed by ten. It was the simplest routine. Even his meals were absolutely regular in quantity. He enjoyed food, when he let himself. He was as rigid with himself as though he were his own physician. None of us remember a single lapse or any indulgence. And his magnificent body remained a miracle of vigor, his eyes clear and vivid, and his skin, where it was not burned, as white and smooth as a little child's. Nor was his face tortured by lines. He was never wrinkled, even when he grew really old. His high smooth brow was still tranquil, his lean cheeks unlined. Such it was to have a mind untroubled and sure of itself. He was a perfectly happy soul, living in a strong and subdued body.

So he went unscathed through sickness and disease everywhere about him and remained whole and untouched. If he had a little malaria, a dash of quinine instantly restored him, so quick to respond was his healthy body. And as time went on he seemed to build up his own immunity and never had malaria at all. Time after time he went into famine areas to do relief work and others came down with typhus, but never he. Smallpox he escaped, though even he wondered at that, because for years he did not think of being vaccinated. "It slipped my mind," he said calmly. Only once was he desperately ill in all the years of his youth and maturity and that was from a sunstroke, caught on a fiery July day in Shanghai. For six weeks he lay unconscious, fighting his battles in his dreams, arguing with his enemies, the missionaries and the mandarins, and planning for new fields of work. To enlarge, to expand, to reach more souls—that was his endless passion in his delirium as in his life.

But unconsciously he felt the shortening of his years, for in the decade after he was fifty he worked as he had never worked. His Testament was finished and he was revising edition after edition. He was on innumerable committees, for his energy and forthrightness were admired and trusted even by those who hated him. There have not been too many like him in that respect.

To be a missionary is an acute test of integrity. For a missionary has no supervision. He lives among a few equals, the other missionaries, and a great many whom he feels his inferiors, the natives. His governing board is thousands of miles away—there is no one to see how many hours he works or whether he is lazy and self-indulgent. And the climate, the small but absolute security of salary, the plentiful number of cheaply paid servants, all make laziness easy, and a man's fellows are loath to tell of him even if they see, and the Chinese converts are helpless for they do not know to whom to complain. There is no one beyond the missionary for them. These stand next to God and are supreme in authority, having the right to give or withhold funds which mean life.

A missionary's integrity, therefore, must be beyond that of any other white man's, and sometimes, perhaps even more often than not, it is. For the Standard Oil or the British-American Tobacco Company can check sales lists and have the solid proof of money received, but even a list of church members means nothing at all—not in China, where the gift of tongues is universal, and where histrionic power is a common possession. The newest convert can, after a minimum amount of rehearsal, rise before the congregation and make a prayer so rich and fluent, so copious in spiritual experience that it would be the envy of any American bishop. Missionaries are human enough, God knows, and so do the Chinese. Doubtless most of them struggle against laziness as we all do, and some give up to it, but most of them struggle along. But Andrew was a flame of integrity. It was impossible to imagine him struggling. He was always in complete command of himself. His duty was done to the last ounce of its demand. Even his enemies never questioned that burning integrity. As for the Chinese, they trusted him like children. If he said a thing they knew it would come true. "He says it," was good collateral anywhere. Curiously —or was it curiously?—the fact that the Chinese loved him and trusted him increasingly did not make the missionaries love him better. But then it is quite true he always took sides with the Chinese. He believed, for instance, in a day too early for such belief, that the Chinese and American workers should have equal power of decision regarding policies of the work. He took no stock in the idea that the white men ought to stand by each other and maintain a fiction of rightness and authority before the Chinese. Such notions in his day were heresies.

So the idea of age came as an absurdity. It is difficult to remember when it began. He was making his long journeys as he always had, examining applicants for church membership, examining school curriculums, holding conferences with preachers and teachers, going incredible distances on foot and horseback, by rail and by water. In these later years he met with little physical hazard because he was so known and loved.

Once in the hills of Kiangsu he was taken by bandits and they asked him who he was. When he told them they let him go and gave him back his purse they had taken.

"We have heard of you in many places," they said simply. "You do good deeds."

Andrew, seeing them in such a mood, stayed a while to preach to them and tell them the story of the robber who hung beside Christ on the cross and was received into heaven when he repented. He must have preached rather long, for some of the young ones grew restive, but the old bandit chieftain shouted at them—and Andrew told this himself with a grin—"Be still! Don't you see the man is trying to get to heaven by this task he has set himself to save our souls? We must help him by waiting until he is through."

So he compelled them to stay and Andrew gave them each copies of the Gospel tracts he had written and came home in much triumph, confident forever after that he would meet some of those bandits in heaven. For, he argued, he had been sent to save them.

"Weren't you afraid?" we inquired of him.

There was, he admitted, a nasty moment when one of the young bandits had a knife at his stomach and was making unpleasant screwing motions. "But it was certainly very nice afterwards," he said. "They sat so nicely and listened—they were really very nice men, in spite of their unfortunate calling."

There was something puzzling about Andrew. He seemed sometimes almost a fool for naïveté. One could not be sure that he really understood the situations in which he found himself. But he was God's fool.

When did it begin to occur to us that even his magnificent and unfailing body must break? I think it was when the Chinese began to say to us, "He must not rise so early and travel so far and work so hard. Persuade him to rest and take a little more food. He is no longer young."

Not young! We looked at Andrew. He seemed the same. He pshawed away any change in his routine. No, he wouldn't take any more vacation. Why should he go into the coolness of mountains and rest when his Chinese colleagues could not?

It was after a long and particularly hot summer, which he had spent alone, that we noticed a weariness about him that had not been, a slackening that could not be defined, because he worked as hard as ever. But he did not work so eagerly as he had always done and he was sometimes too tired to eat at all. There was one evening, for instance, when he came home very late, having taken a much later train than usual from an out-station. He made no explanation, however. Instead he went upstairs and bathed and shaved freshly and came down to supper looking unusually well in a white suit of Chinese linen.

Something disturbed him, though—we could all see it —and when he was pressed he said shamefacedly and with a shade of bewilderment that was a little touching, "I don't know how I could have done it. But I went to sleep on the train and slept beyond my station. When I woke the train was at the end of the line and I was too late for the service, so I could only turn around and come home."

It was so unlike him to oversleep that we searched him for something wrong. But he seemed himself, after all. Then a week later he came back from a journey with a slight paralysis of the face—a drooping lid to his left eye, a twisted corner of the left side of his mouth. This was serious. He could not articulate quite clearly, but we understood that he had sat up all night in the coolie class to save money.

Carie was angry with anxiety. "Save money!" she cried. "And what of yourself? What's the good of a dollar if you're dead?"

He looked at her speechless, humble with his state. The doctor was called and he said a rest was necessary and at once. Andrew's furlough was years overdue. Indeed he had quite forgotten about furloughs, and Carie had made up her mind she would never cross the sea again anyway. But the youngest child was ready for college and she pressed upon Andrew the need of someone's taking her back to America, knowing that unless she could make it seem his duty to go he never would, especially when after a few days in bed his face straightened to normal again and he pshawed over the idea of more rest. But she prevailed, and exactly forty years after he had left his own country, Andrew went back again for what was to be his last visit. For he made up his mind to that, fearful lest he die away from China. His illness, slight as it was, had made him realize his mortal body. He would go to America but only for a few months—he did not want to be away from China where he had lived his life and where his friends were and, most dear of all, his work. He went off, very resolutely, standing quite still by the rail of the ship's deck, staring at the fading outlines of the Shanghai Bund.

"I'll be back in exactly four months from today," he said. He had already bought his return ticket and had it pinned with a safety pin inside his "cholera belt," a strip of flannel he wore about his waist night and day.

We were not able to comprehend from his letters all that he felt about America. There were hints that it was an entirely new country, not in the least the sort of place he and Carie had known and which they had for nearly half a century away from it called "home." Carie, reading his scanty short sentences aloud looked up to say, "Andrew can tell less than any man in creation, but I never knew him to tell as little about anything as he does now about home. It doesn't seem worth going at all."

When in four months to the day we met Andrew in Shanghai, looking very well, we all cried at him together, "What is America like now? You didn't tell us anything."

"I didn't dare begin," he answered a trifle grimly. Then he added, "There were things I didn't want to put down on paper."

"What things?" Carie demanded at once.

"All kinds of things," he answered.

Bit by bit we pried out of him the salient facts of an amazing post-war America. Everybody was drunk, he said over and over—well, practically everybody. Andrew was no teetotaller, not with St. Paul advising Timothy to take a little wine for his stomach's sake. And he used to say meditatively that it must mean something that every race of humanity on earth had some kind of liquor. Carie flew at him when he talked thus—she had her own reasons for hating liquor. Besides, nothing started her off like quoting St. Paul. We listened solemnly while Andrew told us of drinking and smoking—even the women.

"The women are the worst," he said guardedly, and after a pause he said diffidently, "I scarcely know how to tell you about the women in America."

"What do you mean?" Carie demanded with sternness.

He hesitated, being always the shyest of men where women were concerned.

"It's the way they dress now," he went on. We waited. "They wear hardly any skirts," he said quickly.

"Andrew!" cried Carie.

"It's true," he said. "Everywhere I went the women had dresses up to their knees. It was awful."

"Don't tell me my sisters did it!" Carie exclaimed.

"Well, theirs were better," he admitted, and then repeated with a sort of gloomy reminiscent pleasure, "Yes, everywhere I went they had all their dresses up to their knees."

We stared at him, shocked into silence.

"Their legs were awful," he said, remembering. "Big and fat, long and thin—"

Carie could not bear it. "It does seem you needn't have looked at them," she said with severity.

"I couldn't help it," he said simply. "They were lying around everywhere."

We sat in silence, overcome by the idea of a ruined America. It was Carie who brought us back. She rose briskly.

"Well, you're back safely anyhow," she said. But somehow she made us feel it had been a narrow escape.

Later from various relatives we heard bits about Andrew in America. He had expressed himself very freely, we gathered, on almost every part of life. "Andrew acted as though he didn't know he wasn't in a heathen country," Christopher the Methodist wrote.

"So I was," said Andrew grimly in parenthesis, reading the letter. He looked up. "Chris doesn't preach strong enough sermons," he went on. "I heard him—you can't save souls by a lot of soft talk."

"Andrew looked very well," his sister Rebecca wrote. "He's as stubborn as ever."

"What did you do at Becky's house?" Carie inquired.

"It was the hottest day of summer and she wanted me to wear my long coat when I preached," Andrew said guardedly.

Carie looked at him, speechless. There had been a sharp, short argument over the frock coat when he left for America, and she had put it into his bulging suitcase. But after he had gone, when she was putting away the winter things, she found it hanging in his closet hidden behind his overcoat. She had been exasperated, but helpless.

"He's in the middle of the Pacific or I'd go right after him with it in my hand," she declared, her eyes snapping.

Andrew looked away now. "I wouldn't have worn it if I'd had it," he said. "I wore a white suit as I do here when it's hot."

"But nobody wears white suits in America!" Carie cried.

"Then I was the only sensible man in the nation," he retorted.

Well, we never could do anything with him. And he came back from his four months' rest feeling as strong and eager as ever and plans were sparkling out of his eyes and in the eagerness of his step. He was nearly seventy years old, but he looked fifty. His hair was greying, but it was thick on his head, and his moustache and bushy eyebrows were as red as ever and his eyes as icy blue. He was at home only one day and was off again with Ma the Christian, sailing joyously down the Grand Canal to tour his field and talk over everything that had happened since he left. Ma, twenty years younger, looked older than Andrew. He had in recent years developed a slow chronic tuberculosis of the lungs which kept him bone thin and made his eyes more burning and hollow than ever and his black hair look dead and dry. His hands were the hands of death, they were so shadow-like. Andrew plied him with condensed milk and raw eggs and a great deal of prayer, and the disease seemed stationary at least, although Andrew regularly remarked, "Ma will never pull through another winter." But he did, to live in the end years beyond Andrew, still with that cough of his. Something else than food and flesh kept him living.

Looking back over the span of Andrew's life it can be seen that this tour was the height of his life. It was the hour when all his life's work lay before him in full fruit, organized, operating, in large measure self-governing and self-supporting. He had always believed, in opposition to the policy of many missionaries, that the Chinese Christians should have full powers of self-government. They should, he said, be free of all rules and domination from the missionaries. He even went so far, heretic as he was, to say that if the forms of church government and creeds found in the various Western denominations did not suit them, the Chinese should make those which would fit their own souls, only bearing always in mind the Holy Trinity.

Such ideas made him loved by the Chinese and hated by many a missionary with an autocratic turn of mind, and most missionaries are autocrats. Andrew was himself, for that matter, for he knew he was right.

That autumn, then, was the height of his life. The

work had gone well while he was away, and he spent the long shining autumn days, from morning until darkness, in surveying his field. I know that the beauty of the countryside struck him with unusual clarity, for more often than ever before he spoke of the splendor of the harvest fields of rice. It was a good year and there would be no famine that winter and such confidence alone brought exhilaration. He hated to preach to starving people, lest they were listening for the sake of a little food rather than for salvation.

And it was a glorious country. The wide golden Yangtse flowed through its midst and sprang aside into hundreds of canals and streams that fed the most fertile valleys in China. Beyond the valleys were rolling bamboo-covered hills where old temples had stood for hundreds of years, and where drowsy priests smiled amicably when Andrew told them their gods were false. He always felt he had to tell them, not rudely but with a twist of humor.

He would point his stick at a bowl of food set before a god and remark gently, "I suppose he will eat that when nobody is looking?" And the priest would grin and nod or he would say comfortably, "He sees it and takes the essence of it and he does not mind if we poor priests take the worthless matter that's left and eat it."

Then Andrew would go on and talk a little about the true God, and the priest would listen and murmur,

"Every man has his own god, and to each his is the true one, and there are enough for us all."

But such tolerance did not suit Andrew. He was fond of quoting a Chinese proverb which says that around the mouth of hell the priests cluster thickly.

Through the valleys and beyond the hills ran the old cobbled roads, worn into ruts by squeaking wheelbarrows —it is bad luck for a wheelbarrow to have no squeak, so that every man encourages it in his own—and smooth with the short-stepped trotting feet of donkey caravans. Andrew had always a strong feeling for the little grey donkeys of China—indeed, there was a softness in him for all animals, but particularly for horses and donkeys, and at home for a cat. There was something about a cat by the hearth which he liked. When he was old he sat by the hour with the cat spread across his knees, stroking it gently. And when he was younger he would often delay his hurrying trips to blame a donkey driver because the beast's back was sore from overloading. He knew, he said, that God's plan provided no place for beasts in heaven, and man ought therefore to take especial care that they had at least a comfortable life upon earth, since there was no other for them.

Everywhere he went he was welcomed and loved. It was an experience to travel with him and see how for hundreds of miles he was known and loved. "The Old Teacher has come back!" people shouted to each other from doorway to doorway. "Old Teacher, Old Teacher!" people called to him, and little street children trotted behind him to his great pleasure and followed him into chapels and crowded the front benches, enduring his long sermons with fair patience until they were over and they could roar out a hymn, which they delighted to do, and clamor for a Bible picture. The picture of Christ they always examined with particular closeness. Once a small dirty urchin, looking at a picture in the middle of the sermon, interrupted Andrew. "Why, this Jesus looks like a Chinese except his nose is too big. His nose is like your nose, but his skin is like mine!"

And Andrew, who would have tolerated nothing like this from one of his own children, smiled and explained that indeed Jesus Christ was not a white man, and went on with his sermon. He had infinite patience with the people to whom he felt himself sent.

Everywhere he went that autumn the churches seemed peculiarly prosperous. The members were not of the poorest class any more. They were rich silk and tea merchants, owners of restaurants and shops, and they gave money willingly for the upkeep of the church. So far as eye could see, everything was in order among them. The services of the church were performed regularly and the churches were crowded. The schools, too, were doing well. The old days when the missionary had to bribe people to send their children to Christian schools by giving them everything, even food and clothes, were over. There could be tuition fees nowadays, when Western learning was coming into fashion and even the government schools were being reorganized and the old classics were being set aside for science and mathematics and most especially English. Everybody wanted to learn English. If a boy knew English maybe he could get a job in the Standard Oil or the tobacco company, or maybe he could even get a scholarship from the Boxer Indemnity to go to America and study. Little village boys with a turn for letters began to dream of going to America as their fathers used to dream of passing the old imperial examinations and becoming mandarins.

Not that Andrew ever encouraged any boy to go to America. It would be the ruin of him, he used to declare. America wasn't what it was, what with the automobiles and nobody going to church. He saw somewhere the figures of the year's deaths by automobile accidents in the United States and he never forgot it. He used to quote it solemnly when people talked of progress and motor cars. "Thirty thousand people a year, and most of them in hell! That's the sort of people who drive like that, undoubtedly."

Once a flippant child remarked, "So many the fewer souls to bother to save, then," to which he replied sternly, "I would not even want to see a Baptist go to hell by way or an automobile!" He was thinking of the one-eyed missionary.

But then China was his heart's home. He gave up any thought of other lands, knowing that here he would live out his life and here die. That autumn he traveled over the roads and stopped at cities and towns and the welcoming calls of the people warmed his heart. They made a sort of gala occasion of that tour of his, feeling him safely returned. He passed his sixty-ninth birthday, which made him seventy according to the Chinese reckoning, whereby a child at birth is already a year old, and they prepared feasts for him, gave him scrolls gilded and inscribed with words of praise and wide banners of red satin embroidered with letters of black velvet, and last, the insignia of an honored official, a huge red satin panoply borne aloft on a tall pole. He was much embarrassed with it and pleased, too, and came triumphantly home with all his gifts. Carie was put to it to know what to do with so much magnificence of scarlet satin in the plain little mission house, and at last she put everything away in the little round-backed trunk in the attic. There was no place for honor and glory in that self-sacrificing house. Later the trunk fell into the hands of revolutionary soldiers, who divided the shining stuff among them, snatching at it with dirty claws of hands and screeching at each other in quarreling over it. Andrew was relieved to have it gone, and Carie was in the grave by then, and the only one of us all who was safe.

Andrew came home after his three months' tour in a high serenity of happiness. He had always been happy and zestful for his life. His rare fits of melancholy were always cured by work, and his work could never be done. All through the years his soul had been borne along on the lift of his ever enlarging plan, and again and again his own spirit was refreshed by the ecstasy of the knowledge that some other soul had found that source of reason for life which he found in God.

There is no way to explain that ecstasy in Andrew. The only thing I have seen like it is the ecstasy of a father beholding his child for the first time. There was a paternal tenderness in Andrew over every soul who came up to him for baptism. There was a look upon his face, a brooding joy when he lifted his hand to bless the newborn soul, which the children of his flesh never saw when he looked upon them. For Andrew's kin were not those of the blood, but those of the spirit, and he was knit in some mystic fashion to every soul he felt he had brought to salvation. By such ecstasies was he renewed.

But even we had never seen him in the exaltation of that autumn. It had not occurred to him that he was growing old or could ever be old. He never had looked at his face in a mirror to see what it was—Mrs. Pettibrew had settled that long ago when he was a boy in West Virginia. His hair had grown grey late and was not yet white, and his face was as ruddy and his eyes as clearly blue as ever. He was almost jocular with youth, cracking his dry jokes, laughing easily his "haw!" of laughter, because he was so happy. He measured happiness by the success of his work, by the eagerness of souls crowding to be saved—else why should they want to become members of the church?—and his work was growing and there were souls by the hundred.

"What are you thinking?" we asked him one Sunday morning at breakfast when he put down his cup and seemed to be listening, his eyes shining, his whole face alight.

"It came to me suddenly that in thousands of homes today those who were heathen are preparing, young and old, to worship God, and in hundreds of churches and chapels they will sit and listen and pray." It was the top of his life.

X

A LITTLE while before this there had come to the station which Andrew made his home a younger missionary and then two others. Indeed, after years of wanting to be alone in his field, Andrew decided it would be well to have a young man or two. He liked young men and had always had a half-joking, half-paternal way with these three, not taking them very seriously, teasing them sometimes about their mistakes in Chinese. There was that time, for instance, when one of them, thinking to use a festival day for the glory of God, brought it into his sermon. It was the birthday of the Flower God, or Hwa Shen, as the people called the god, and the young missionary preached eloquently against the god, adjuring the people not to worship him. But he used the wrong tones in the two syllables, and thereby all unconsciously transformed them into two others, meaning peanuts. The people sat in solemn bewilderment, not understanding why this American became so excited in pleading with them not to worship peanuts, which they never had worshipped, and Andrew sat choking with silent laughter. It was too good a joke not to tell, and he told it perhaps a trifle too often. And it was not a joke easy for a proud young missionary to bear. And there were others. Andrew knew a great deal and he was an acknowledged scholar in Chinese, and he had spent most of his life in China. It is a little cruel to laugh at the young, but Andrew did not think of that.

Then there was his stubbornness. He had been used to his own way for so many years. When the three young men voted against him in the solemn station meetings of four voting men and four non-voting women, Andrew was only amused. What—let these young fellows with the milk of their mother seminary still wet on their lips tell him what to do? They quoted mission rules to him concerning majority votes, but he pshawed and gave his haw of laughter and did as he pleased.

It was Carie who fought for him, really—Carie with her French shrewdness which perceived that even the prophets plotted against each other. She used to say, troubled, "They are going to oust you one of these days, Andrew—see if they don't!"

"Oh, pshaw, they can't!" he would reply absently, his mind on his plans. He never knew how often when he was not there she defended him and by the very energy of her tongue, kept them quiet. There is that enmity between young and old.

It was when Andrew came home in such triumph, in such fullness of strength and success, that they came one day and told him of the new rule the mission had made while he was away.

"What rule?" he asked amiably. The mission was always making rules—a man would be busy just keeping up with them.

"A new retirement rule has been passed," said the eldest of the three. He had once been a clerk in a department store and God called him out of it to go to China and save souls, but he had never quite got over his feeling about rules. They came down from above. He went on solemnly. "The rule is that a missionary retires at the age of seventy."

They waited for Andrew to grasp it, these righteous young priests before an old son of God who had grown uncouth with his years of hardship and rough travel and living far from the cities. Andrew was no drawing-room figure, for all the distinction he had of a high bearing and a learned serenity and fastidious neatness. He never troubled himself to be thoughtful of anyone in small ways. No one ever saw him pick up a woman's handkerchief, for instance, or rise to give her his seat. And tact he scorned utterly as a subterfuge and a weakness. He stared from one to the other. Striplings—that's what they were!

"Pshaw!" he said loudly. It had just occurred to him that he was practically seventy years old. He grew very calm—even kind. What could these young men understand? They were so young. Why, there were a great many things which he himself was only just now beginning to know and to be able to do! China was a land where age added influence and benefit. The people respected him for being old—that is, older.

But it was Carie who fought his battle, Carie with her quick tongue and fiery sense of justice and flying temper. She had been sitting unseen in the next room. They were afraid of her and had told Andrew at the door they wanted to see him alone.

"I didn't trust them the instant I heard them say that," she exclaimed, telling of it. She rose, overturning her enormous sewing box in her haste. We found buttons and spools of thread under things for days. She swept into the other room, her eyes fairly crackling, her very hair electric. We knew how she looked—had we not seen Carie in battle?

"What are you saying?" she cried. She never bothered about soft speaking at such times. "You will get out of my house! There's not one of you fit to—to wear his old shoes! You soft-living, ease-loving— He works harder than any of you! Seventy, is he? Get out!" They had gone.

So much she told us she said—"and a good deal more," said Andrew drily. He did not appreciate Carie's battles for his sake—after all, a woman—"I can really look out for myself," he said to her gently, but with firmness.

"You think you can, but you can't," she retorted. "They get ahead of you."

"They don't," he replied.

Their conversations were always made up largely of contradictions.

"They do," she said. He rose abruptly and went out.

"Andrew has no notion of the way people really are," she said when the door was shut. "He's so far above plotting himself that he doesn't know it's in the world. And somehow being Christians doesn't cure them of it." Carie was somewhat of a pessimist about human nature. But it was true that Andrew was guileless and blind.

Andrew said he would not worry about that retirement rule. Nobody could retire him—not until God called him to death.

"They could stop your salary and drive you out of this house," Carie said.

"They wouldn't do that," he said peaceably, and added, "If they did, there would be Chinese who would give us shelter and food."

It was the Chinese who saved him, though. When they heard of the new rule there was such consternation as never was. The Old Teacher! Because he was old! But in China the old were to be honored, to be humored and given their way, not put aside for the very thing that gave them dignity and meaning. Besides, who wanted these young Americans? They were used to the Old Teacher and he understood them and they would have no one else to be their superior. Delegations of courteous but determined Chinese appeared and presented documents signed by long lists of names. In the end Andrew went on unretired and more triumphant than ever.

Looking back, I can understand how these young priests did not savor such an uproar about an old man whose ways of working were not their ways. It could not have been pleasant to hear that they were not loved as he was loved, nor welcomed as he was. Nor did they realize how many years it had taken him to win that love—how much persecution he had borne and how steadfastly he had visited the sick and stayed by the dying and how often upheld a struggling soul. None of us know how often he did these things, for he never told us. They were simply part of his work. Most of all the Chinese loved him because he knew no color to a man's soul and he took the part of the yellow man again and again against the white man—the lonely convert's side, the poorly paid native preacher's side, against the arrogant priest, the superior missionary.

But those young men were quite sincere. They thought that Andrew was a hindrance to the work, to the sound development of the church. He received members into the church without adequate preparation and examination, they said, visiting him again and again to remonstrate with him.

"I receive, by the authority of my office under God alone, such souls as profess repentance and accept Jesus Christ as their savior," he said with his high look.

It was not enough, they said. These professions were often hypocritical. It meant there were many on the church rolls who should not be there. It made for an unsound organization.

"God will purge them out," Andrew said with confidence.

It was not enough, they said. There were hypocrites even among the leaders. The native preachers themselves were not all true—perhaps most of them under Andrew's loose supervision were guilty of much. There were hints of corruption, of fees accepted, of mishandling church funds, of secret concubinage.

They sat, the three righteous young men, before Andrew and Carie and made their charges. For Andrew let Carie come in now. He was beginning to grow bewildered. The young priests sat facing these two white-haired old people—Andrew's hair seemed to whiten in a week, and Carie's hair had for years been a heap of feathery snow. They had all their facts and figures and Andrew had never been good at keeping figures. He knew roughly how many souls had been saved and how many churches and schools he had and in general how much money he could spend. But these young men knew everything about his field. They had toured it all while he was in America, examining, asking questions, making notes. They had hirelings of their own go and seek out enemies of the church in each town and ask questions about the personal lives of those whom Andrew trusted. When they accused Ma, his close friend, he rose up trembling. "Now I know you're—you're absolutely wrong," he stammered. "I would trust Ma before I'd trust you—or myself."

They smiled. "Perhaps that's been your chief mistake—you seem to have trusted everybody."

The little thin one spoke. "You can't trust the Chinese."

Andrew came to life with a roar. A few times in his life he lost his gentleness and his voice came out of him like a great trumpet.

"If you believe that, why have you come to save them?" he shouted. "How can you save souls if you despise them? Shame on a follower of Jesus Christ who despises any man, however sinful!" He was on his feet, shouting. Carie sat by, silent for once, because he did not need her. He sat down again, suddenly—those moments of his were short, and terrible. He was silent an instant and began again more quietly, "It is necessary to believe in those to whom we have been sent. A soul cannot be won except through belief and patient understanding. I had rather accept some souls who are insincere than refuse one who is true. God will discern, He who sends rain upon just and unjust."

But there were the facts and the figures, there were proofs. They produced certain absolute proofs.

It went on for days, for weeks, for months, the steady

undermining of all his work, the devaluation of all which he had so labored to build up. He stoutly refused to believe any of it, but he began to be distressed. He and Carie argued endlessly. Some of what they said was true, she said—it was better to acknowledge what was true and try to correct what wrong there was. But he would acknowledge nothing. Her arguments always strengthened him to opposition, and on opposition his energies blazed freshly. He held everything exactly as it was, went on receiving new members, refused to dismiss anyone—no, not Lin whom they accused of opium smoking, nor Chang who they said was running a big tea house with sing-song girls on the proceeds of the church. He had to have more proofs than he had been shown before he would dismiss a man. Besides, there was Ma, steadily denying everything. He had always believed Ma.

What would have happened if Carie had lived I do not know. She was always beside him, defending him in public, and in private moving him to decisions, to energies, to defenses and fresh determinations by her restless mind, approving and criticizing together.

But Carie died that next autumn. He knew she had not been well, but then she had not been well for years and he had scarcely known it because her will was so large and so indomitable, her body so negligible. She took no consideration of herself and expected none from others. He had an idea that women were often ill—it seemed so in this climate. Besides, Carie never wanted him near when she was ill. It was inconvenient to have her ill, but he did not see anything he could do for her, and anyway there were two daughters in his house. She had been in bed a good deal, but he had been so harassed in his work, so worried—and then one day he saw she was very ill indeed.

At once the trouble with the young missionaries was less important. Carie begged him to go on, but he felt it his duty to delay going away from home until the doctor had made his examination. When the doctor made his report there was no question of going away. She was mortally ill.

When Andrew knew that unless God wrought a miracle Carie's life was soon to end, his first thought was of her soul. For once he asked no miracle and seemed to expect none. He was restless with anxiety over her soul. He felt he ought to speak to her.

"I have never felt entirely certain about your mother's soul," he said to Carie's daughter one morning.

Carie's daughter replied with a touch of sharpness, "Her soul is all right!"

Andrew did not answer. He went slowly upstairs to Carie's room. But when he tried to speak to her, she suddenly was impatient and flouted him in a way she had not been able to do for days.

"You go along and save your heathen," she said, and

her eyes flashed for a moment. So he gave it up, after all, and Carie went on dying as she was.

When the end was very near, the nurse they had got from Shanghai came running into his study where he was working on a revision of the Testament—by some strange coincidence he was working on the crucifixion scene and the solemnity of death had already filled him.

"There's a change," the nurse cried, and he rose and followed her upstairs. He could not hurry—he was strangely afraid. Carie dying! It brought death too near. He had stood at many deathbeds, and some of his children had died, but death had not seemed near to him until now.

He went into the room he and Carie had shared for many years, where she now lay in the big double bed alone.

She was unconscious. He was almost glad, for he would not have known what to say to her. It was strange he could think of nothing he would have said. So he stood gravely at the foot of the bed, waiting. The room was full of an awful solemnity as her breath came, caught in her breast, and went out of her with a great sigh, to come no more. In the endless silence he turned and went downstairs, back to his study, and shut the door.

He did not speak of her again, and none of us saw him weep. Whether he was widowed or not, none of us knew. He took no part in any of the last preparations and when we called him to her funeral he dressed himself carefully and went with us. He stood tearless beside her grave, his face set in utter gravity, his eyes sealed in gravity. But he said nothing, and after it was all over he went back to his study again and shut the door. Carie's daughter, yearning over him, passed by the window, to see if he were grieving there alone. But he was working over the pages of the Testament, the Chinese brush in his hand, painting the characters one by one down the page. It was impossible to go in, and she went on upstairs into the bedroom, now his alone, to straighten it for him. Upon the bed lay the frock coat. He had taken it down, pondering whether he would wear it for Carie's sake. But he had not worn it, after all, and it lay there upon the bed, and Carie's daughter took it and hung it up again.

He never mentioned Carie's name again as long as he lived unless a direct question were asked of him, and no one could tell if he grieved. And he never once visited her grave. But something broke in him, some strength of stubbornness. There was no one at home to contradict him, praise him, blame and scold him into energy. The house was very still with only one daughter left, and the other married and gone up the river to live. He had lived always in a routine and it did not occur to him to change it, but sometimes he wanted to change it and could not. Carie had always protested against routine; she loved change and different days. Opposing her volatility, routine had seemed important to him, and valuable, and the only way to accomplish anything—now it seemed less valuable, when there was no one to disturb it.

In the midst of his bewilderment the righteous young men were at him again, and Carie could not rise from her grave to battle for him. In the silent house he listened to their certainties, and for the first time in his life doubt began to creep in. Perhaps they were right—perhaps nothing he had done was any use. He put his hand to his forehead in his old gesture of bewilderment, and Carie was not there to cry out, "Not one of you is fit to step into his old shoes!" And they had proofs of everything now—bills for opium stamped with the church seal, signed confessions, sworn statements. Everything was shaking and tumbling about him. Carie was gone and the daughter was a young girl, filled with her own loneliness. There was no one to guide him by telling him to do something he did not want to do and would not; to make him believe in himself again. In this one moment of fumbling and mistrust, the righteous young men put before him something to sign—some sort of promise to turn over his field to them, so that for the sake of the honor of the church they could purify the work. Without knowing what he did, he signed the paper and gave away his work.

All during the winter he stayed at home in a sort of stupor of dismay. He was growing old—they had made him believe it now. He grew very white and, if possible, thinner. He worked a while each day on his translation, and when the weather was fine enough he went to a street chapel to preach. But when before had Andrew stopped for weather? The source in him was failing. Even when some of his faithful converts came to beg him not to give them up, he shook his head helplessly. "I signed something or other," he said with a heavy sigh. He never was sure just what the paper had said, but he knew it took everything away from him. And Ma, who might have helped him, was low that winter with a fresh attack of tuberculosis.

Then spring came. Carie had said to her daughters, "Look out for spring. About the first of April he gets hard to manage. It won't matter if he's eighty, he'll want to get away over the country and behind the hills preaching." When the willows budded in early April and the peach trees bloomed and the wheat was green and farmers were busy about their land, one day he lifted up his head. He smelled the new air. Suddenly he put down his brush and got up and went out of his study to find his youngest daughter, who was now the woman in his house.

"Get my things ready," he commanded her.

"Something came over me," he said, telling of it years later. "I saw I had been a fool."

In a few hours he was on his way on his ancient white horse, riding over the old familiar cobbled roads, over the smooth paths into the hills. And with every mile strength came back to him. "An amazement filled me," he wrote in that story of his. "I saw that I had been in a sinful despair. I dismounted from my beast and going away a little into the privacy of a bamboo grove, I tied the beast and knelt and besought God for forgiveness for the sin of despair. And God heard me and I was delivered and never again did He suffer me to so lose Him."

By the time he reached his first village church he was in a fine anger at the three righteous young men and beyond weariness.

But it was a sad business. He found as he went from place to place that the young men had been very busy. Everything was reorganized. The Chinese preachers whom he had trained and trusted were for the most part gone—"dismissed," he used to say over and over again, "without a particle of real proof and only on rumor. Rumor! Christ was crucified on a rumor and by those who called themselves righteous!"

A fury of hatred filled him as he went about his ruined field. Some of the churches he found shut and the doors sealed, the schools closed. When he came home he went to the young men to demand an explanation. "We found such corruption," they said, "that the only hope was to close everything, scatter the members, and wait and begin again."

And the members were scattered indeed. New, unknown voices were preaching and a few strangers sat and listened half-heartedly. Everything was gone—his whole life's work swept away.

But anger was a strength to him and a healing. He gathered himself together. He would begin again. God would give him years. He would search out his old converts and build new churches out of them—not Presbyterian churches, not organizations subject to the dominations and whims of white men, but native independent churches, using no money but their own, self-supporting, self-governing. He began to plan and with planning despair was gone and after a while anger was gone, and once more he was happy.

And so the search began for the souls he had saved and lost and now was seeking again. He went about in village and town and countryside all that spring and summer, and Ma was better once more in the heat, and the two of them went together searching. Some souls they never found. They had disappeared in the purging. Others they found returned to their old gods, and some they found wavering and not knowing what to do and these were glad to come back to their Old Teacher and were joyful to see him again. And there were others, enough to comfort and reassure him, who had remained true, worshipping God in their homes when the doors of churches were sealed. These were the nucleus of the new church Andrew was to build, the church independent of the foolishness of denominations and the vagaries of men. These were they who were to look straightly to God. They met together in the poorest places, in the tiny living-room of a farmhouse, in the earth-floored room of a country inn. But Andrew fired them to independence. He was very happy.

The three young men found out what he was doing. They had hirelings of their own who brought them stories. Andrew, they said, was dividing the church. He was causing dissension. An independent native church! It was heresy.

When he came home they waited on him in a body and put before him the paper he had signed. But he was strong by now. He only pshawed, and refused to look at it.

"I signed it under compulsion," he declared. "It's not even legal. I'll swear to that before the consul, if you like."

He was free of them all once more, free of everything. But he was old and they were young, and there were things they could do to him, though he forgot them in his old high humor. God's work was yet to be done. God would triumph—but meanwhile he was working his body as fiercely as he had in his youth. He pshawed aside every remonstrance from his daughter. And the young men were about to put on him the pressure of mission authority. He could be removed completely, sent back to America not to return, retired to die. His young daughter grew afraid.

There was not one of Carie's children into whom she had not poured her blood. Not one of them was her equal, but they were all fighters and afraid of no man. And her blood stirred in them now to fight for Andrew. He must be rescued and kept happy. He must never feel old again or set aside and useless. There must always be work for him to do—some sort of God's work, because he would not consider anything else worth doing.

They cast about to find salvation for Andrew in such a way that he could never find out that he had been saved, or ever indeed know he needed saving, proud son of God that he was. Where in the world of young men could he fit? There seemed no place for him. He must be taken away and allowed to work somewhere freely as he always had, for freedom was the only air in which his spirit could live and be.

It happened that part of the fruit of Andrew's life had been helping to build a theological seminary. That passion of his for a literate and educated clergy had gone beyond his training class for his own helpers into the planning and building of a school where young men might go and be trained. It had begun humbly enough many years before, but it had grown through donations, allotments and bequests into a group of brick buildings, sponsored by several denominations of the Protestant church into an institution of some dignity, although its traditions were always conservative. At that they were not narrow enough for Andrew's denomination, and it was for this seminary he had fought for many years with his reiterated slogan, "It's better to stay in and fight than get out and lose all hope of winning." Andrew was not afraid of modernism any more than he was of the devil. It made a good foe, and a good foe always whetted him.

To this institution, then, one of Carie's children turned speculative eyes. It would make a good place for Andrew to work in his old age. He would be doing the sort of thing he loved—teaching young men and associated with them daily, and they would learn from his experience. He would be taken out of the jurisdiction of the righteous three, and if they came near him she could be watchful. Best of all, he would be under her own roof where she could take care of him, for she lived in Nanking where the seminary was. He had grown too thin and his ruddiness had gone and left a sort of transparent whiteness out of which his eyes looked too blue and unearthly. But first she must get the place for him.

It was a task she loathed. She would never have begged for herself—Carie was in her. But she was put to it for Andrew. So she went, in as matter-of-fact a way as she could, to the church dignitary then at the head of the seminary and told the case plainly to him, and when she had finished she made no bones, having planned everything before. "And so you must find something for him to do here where I can look after him and keep him happy and not knowing anything about my coming to you."

The dignitary knew Andrew and knew the redoubtable family and the seven sons. And in his time he had had a passage or two with Carie herself over Andrew. He hesitated and fiddled with a paperweight on his desk. It was, Carie's daughter remembers, a little clay boy on a clay buffalo. "We have no vacancies," he murmured, and added something about wanting younger men.

"Not in China," Carie's daughter said decidedly. "Age won't matter here. Besides, surely there is something he can teach them out of all his years."

It appears there was not. Carie's daughter went away, refused but undefeated. It was not for nothing that she had been brought up in a denomination where women were given no recognized voice. They got what they wanted in other ways.

She returned again and again, until a look of terror came into the dignitary's eyes, and she learned to follow immediately upon the heels of an announcing servant before there were opportunities for any nonsense about being busy.

And the time-worn method of women had its reward. In a moment of extreme weariness he said, toying with the clay buffalo, "Of course we have planned a sort of correspondence course—"

She seized on it. "The very thing!"

"He could be given a couple of able assistants who could do the real work," the dignitary went on.

She laughed secretly. As if Andrew could be kept from real work!

"It wouldn't cost you anything—his salary from home would go on," she said diplomatically.

"It might work," he agreed without fervor.

It was enough to build upon, and she built. She built at both ends. She told Andrew he was going to be invited to the seminary and she saw to it that the letter of invitation was something more than half-hearted and that there were a title and a position as well as work for him to do. He was to be Dean of the Correspondence School —a school that did not exist. "But it will be the more exciting to make it," she tempted Andrew.

And she followed the invitation promptly herself, and Carie in her told her how to persuade Andrew.

"You can run all your independent churches just as easily as ever from my house and there won't be anybody to interfere with you, and you can be teaching at the same time, and you'll have plenty of time to work on your Testament."

It was an alluring picture of freedom, and he could not resist it. It was, he said, an enlargement of his usefulness, and therefore it was doubtless God's will.

"I'm sure it is," Carie's daughter said thankfully.

So the mission bungalow which Carie had made into a home for so long was dismantled. There was a pathetic little sale—there was nothing worth much money, and a few precious things were saved—Carie's desk and her organ, the rocking chair in which she had rocked all her babies, Andrew's books and desk, and a picture or two. They were put on a junk and sent up the river, and the house was empty and the lovely garden left to loneliness. A strange life was to come into it—the wastrel life of the new revolution then rising. When Carie's daughter next saw that house, the last time she was to see it, the house that was so filled with childish memories of hot summer afternoons and Christmas mornings and Carie's voice singing and Andrew coming home, it was a tenement filled with the ruin and waste of revolution. Twenty families of refugees crowded into the rooms Carie had kept so dainty and the plaster was stripped to the laths, and the floors were inches deep in human filth, and the starving people looked out of the holes of windows like desperate dogs. And the garden, where Carie had grown her roses and where lilies had bloomed under the bamboos, had been beaten back to barrenness by the incessant tread of plodding feet. But Carie's eyes were safely shut in her grave, and I am glad for that.

Andrew was to have ten more years to live. He began them happily by disliking at once the room Carie's daughter had given him in her house. She had gone to great pains about that room. First she had chosen the biggest and best room, the one that faced the mountain and the pagoda, into which the sunshine poured cheer. She had furnished it with home things—the rug from Carie's living-room, his own chair, the clock he had wound regularly for forty years, his books in the bookcase—and she made curtains for the windows, very simple white ones, knowing Andrew. She was proud of that room. She ushered him into it.

"The whole house is yours, Father, but this is your own special room."

But it soon appeared that Andrew was uncomfortable. He ranged about the house, looking at various rooms.

"That room of mine," he complained, "it's too big—too much stuff in it—it looks too luxurious."

"You shall have any room you want," she said.

He chose a small room over the kitchen and his things were moved into it. Once more Carie's daughter hung curtains and pictures and spread the rug. Andrew was out when the moving was done, and he made no comment when he came back. But that evening after he had gone up to bed they heard noises prolonged into the night. Carie's daughter went to the door.

"Are you all right?" she called through it.

"Yes," he answered serenely.

She tried the door handle, but it was locked, so after a moment there seemed nothing to do but go away.

The next morning when she went in after he was gone to his day's work she could not believe what she saw. The floor was bare and the curtains were gone and there were no pictures—not even the picture of Carie she had hung upon the wall. And the cushion she had put in the back of his chair to soften its wooden hardness was gone, and the extra mattress she had put to soften the hardness of the single iron bed he had insisted upon buying for himself was gone. She looked under the bed and found the rug and the mattress and in the closet were the curtains and the pictures. The room was a cell, and the sunshine streamed into it mercilessly to show it bare and hideous. But Andrew had arranged it to suit his own heart. A few times in after years Carie's daughter, suffering for its ugliness in a home she tried to make beautiful on what little she had, put curtains at the windows again, small unobtrusive ones, or she slipped in a surreptitious cushion, and any number of times she tried to soften that rigid bed of his with a secret quilt. But Andrew never suffered such things for a day. She always found them put sternly away, folded under the bed or in the closet, and Andrew had his own monastic way to the end.

He took his new work very much for granted and was completely happy. No one crossed him and he lived tremendously. He was busy from early morning until late night. There was constant conference with the men he had chosen to lead the new independent movement. Living cost him nothing these days. He had two good enough suits and saw no need for buying anything for years, if ever, for himself, and he could spend his whole salary on the independent movement. For of course there had to be someone to visit the churches, teach the people and encourage them in plans for expansion. Expansion! It was the old energy of Andrew's life.

I confess that those men from the independent churches who came so regularly to take Andrew's money were not reassuring in their looks. But Andrew could bear no criticism of them. This was the salvaging of his life's work.

"Pshaw, he can't help the way he looks!" he would say when Carie's daughter expressed distaste for a man. "I don't like a pretty man, myself. He's a soundly converted soul and that's the chief thing."

But the soundly converted souls did disconcertingly often look out of amazingly shifty eyes, eyes that would not meet the direct gaze of Carie's daughter, and the hands they put out of their long sleeves were repulsively dirty and eager for money. It is very probable that the three righteous young men were at least partly right, and that Andrew's wheat was badly sown with tares. He was so guileless and hopeful a soul! But he was happy, and Carie's daughter was satisfied.

He was perfectly happy. He came home in the evening exultant with the day, for he loved his work in the seminary. The sight of the young Chinese men who were fitting themselves to go out and preach the Gospel was unfailingly thrilling to his heart. He liked the men set to work with him and went to passionate planning for making a correspondence school of the best sort. He sent all over the world for correspondence school curriculums and took from each what he thought was its best. His New Testament found a new reason for being, too, for without any conceit whatever, Andrew considered his the best and only really intelligible translation into Chinese of the New Testament and in the fullest sense of duty, he put it among the required texts in his new curriculum. When he had everything ready the new school was announced and immediately met with remarkable success. In the course of the ten years Andrew was to see the student roll mount into hundreds and upon it were men from every country in the Orient and some of the South Sea Islands and a few were among Chinese in the United States. Andrew was especially proud of that. All the time he was working for the independent churches, and twice a year he hired a junk—for he had sold his own boat to get money for the new movement—and went out to visit all the members.

So Andrew would not grow old. But it could be seen that his body, in spite of him, was becoming increasingly insufficient for his soul's reach. He came home from every journey spent with exhaustion and white with a whiteness that made his flesh opaque. No sun could make him ruddy in these days. He took on a frosty whiteness that made him seem more unearthly than ever. Carie's daughter begged him to give up the long journeys to the churches, at least, but he would not.

But the day came when he must. He came home unexpectedly one sunny October afternoon, and his daughter saw at once that he was desperately ill. He staggered up the stone steps to the front door, and the sunlight seemed to shine straight through him as though he were a ghost already.

He would answer no questions and she asked none, for she knew him. She put him to bed and sent for the doctor who came and said he was desperately ill with dysentery. Bit by bit as she sat with him through the night she got the story. He had felt he ought to eat the feasts his old and faithful converts prepared for him. "They're poor people," he gasped; "there must have been something they got cheap—but they meant well."

He had returned to his junk and lain there violently ill for three days and two nights.

"Three days!" cried Carie's daughter. "Why didn't you come home or send a messenger to tell us?"

He could not, it appeared. The captain of the junk was a rascal and when he had an old man at his mercy he would not move without money. He took all Andrew had, his watch and pen and all his goods, and only on Andrew's promise that he would never try to punish him in any way did he at last bring him home, nearly dead.

But we were glad the man had not murdered him and thrown his body into the river—glad he had not quite let him die.

For a few days he came very near death, and then came the long difficult turn. The doctor had said Andrew must go to the hospital, but Andrew had refused with what seemed his last breath. He had never been in a hospital and he had no confidence whatever in trained nurses and their morals, he said. He was too weak to cross then, but when he was a very little better the doctor, by means of vast threats, prevailed on him to go to the hospital. But it was no good. Once there, he insisted on watching his schedule continually, half delirious as he was with fever, and he rang his bell every few minutes to remind the nurse he was a very sick man and that his medicine was due at such and such a time—he kept his watch in his hand. As soon as he was fully conscious he insisted on being taken home. That was the time he said, "I have a daughter who has nothing to do but take care of me," and he raised such a storm that he had to be sent home then and there, though he was too sick to sit up.

So Carie's daughter took care of him and he grew well again at last. But he was never quite so well. The illness had frightened him. He sat in an easy chair in a sunny corner of the garden one day with a blanket over his knees and Carie's daughter came to bring him a cup of broth.

He raised solemn blue eyes to hers and said suddenly, "I'm nearly seventy-five years old!"

She looked at him and saw a childlike terror in his eyes. Her heart flew to him, but she resisted the impulse to gather him up like a child in her arms for comfort. He would have been miserably embarrassed at such demonstration. Instead she tucked in his blanket and said, "What's seventy-five? Your family is long lived on both sides. Besides, you're well again, and it's a glorious morning and I've been thinking you ought to revise your book on Chinese idioms. There isn't anything to take its place if you let it go out of print."

"That's true," he exclaimed, pleased. "I've been thinking I ought to do it."

But it was the first fear. He never went out on another tour and the movement for independent churches was never completed. Certain men came and went as long as he lived, and his money went out to them, but Carie's daughter asked no questions. If independent churches made him happier, let him have them, though they were filled with rascals.

The work at the seminary, however, was the ideal work of his old age. Every morning he was up early and impatient for his breakfast and immediately after he was tucked into his comfortable private rickshaw—a victory Carie's daughter had over him—and in his office by eight o'clock. He loved the seminary life, the assemblies where he took his turn at preaching, the coming and going of young men to classes, his own stacks of letters and papers. He felt busy and needed. And young men came to him for advice and confidences, and he listened to their stories of poverty and somehow or other pinched himself yet more to give them aid. Carie's daughter had to watch him or he would have had nothing left. Every week or two she went to his closet and looked over his few garments.

"Where's that knit vest you had for Christmas?" she would demand of him, or she would say, "I can't find but two pair of your woolen socks."

She knew very well that guilty look of his. "One of the young fellows looked awfully cold yesterday—the buildings have no heat and he is too poor to buy a padded coat. Besides, I have my old sweater. I didn't need that fancy vest."

"I can't wear but one pair of socks," he said with impatience. "I'm no centipede, I hope!"

And his rickshaw coolie proudly wore the frock coat which had been such cause for arguments between Carie and Andrew. Andrew sat behind it now with peculiar satisfaction. "The wretched thing is doing somebody some good at last," he said. "The man very sensibly sewed up the tails—I don't know why I didn't think of it long ago."

There was no use in giving him things. We tried to enlarge his meager wardrobe at Christmas and on his birthdays and on any occasion we could use for pretext, but he gave everything away he did not wear at the moment, and it was no pleasure to see a new suit just given him hanging on the small obliterated frame of a divinity student. Andrew was an exasperatingly literal Christian. He even gave away his precious clock to a street chapel on the grounds that he did not need it since he had his watch, although he reserved the right to go and wind it once a week.

But he was not entirely content with his seminary work. His correspondence course did not keep him busy, he said, and so he was touchingly pleased when they gave him a small class or two. No student ever spent such time in preparation as he did. For he considered the work of training men to preach as holy work. It was an extension of his own opportunity to save souls. Through these young men he could reach many another soul.

Even so, he was not content unless he was preaching directly to souls unsaved. So two or three times a week, much to his rickshaw puller's rue, he went into the most crowded parts of the city where in two places he had rented small rooms opening full on the busy street, and there he stood and preached to the people who strayed in to sit a while on a free bench. "He has a hot heart for such an old man," his rickshaw puller used to say, and trudged back and forth with a sigh.

XI

BUT he was not yet to have peace for his work. While he had been living out his zestful days, another storm was rising out of the south, the storm of China's last and greatest revolution.

He had not paid much heed to it. There had been so many wars and revolutions in his day and he had long since refused to go away because he heard a war was threatening. Nobody would hurt him, he always declared. So he had stayed when others fled, coming and going in his usual routine, waiting, perhaps, on the side of a street for an army to march by, but granting no further concession to the eternal upset of China's political life.

And the sight of his tall, white-haired figure coming and going as usual gave the common people comfort and a sense of stability.

"Has the Old Teacher gone?" they asked each other.

"No, he has not gone," was the answer, and they settled themselves again. "If the Old Teacher should go, we would not know where to hide ourselves," they used to say.

But then he never went. And he pshawed the idea that this revolution was different from any other. When people talked of the new Bolshevik influence he refused to grant it importance. Bolsheviks were only people, after all. Besides, "the Chinese will never put up with them," he used to say with confidence. It was one of the secrets of his immense serenity that he always firmly believed anything he said himself.

So as the new revolution swept up from the south and knotted itself into central China and expanded again down the Yangtse River, Andrew regarded it without fear and indeed this time with something of indifference. He had seen so many revolutions come and go, leaving nothing but waste behind, that he had no great optimism. Besides, his mind was turning more and more away from the affairs of men to the one great central meaning of his life, his own work. He had a full sense now of the few years left him, and nothing must turn him aside from that work. He did not hear then the rising of any storm. When news filtered through the countryside of a murdered Catholic priest, he remarked calmly, "Well, he was a Catholic, and they don't like Catholics, I suppose."

When the foreign consuls began to send out warnings, urging women and children and old people to go to Shanghai, since no one could foresee exactly what turn the approaching revolutionary armies would take, it did not occur to him that he could possibly be included among them. What! He run with the women and children?

But then the white people were all sharply divided. Some of them felt no good could possibly come of the new movement, led as it was by the young Western trained Chinese and aided by the Bolshevists. There were others who believed in it and still more who did not know what to think or do. The news of the treatment the white people were receiving in the revolutionary territory was disconcerting, but one could get no proofs or confirmation and mad rumor is at its maddest in China, the land of many tongues and boundless prejudices among men of all colors.

Carie's daughter took sides with the revolutionists. Sun Yat-sen she had admired since her childhood. Carie had taught her that. "Something will come from him," Carie used to say in her tones of confident prophecy, although he was a fugitive most of her life. So when Andrew said he would not go away as the revolutionary armies approached, Carie's daughter made no demur.

Then there came that morning when the consular advice was very strong indeed, amounting as nearly to a command as the representative of a democratic nation may go, that all Americans, women and children and those who were aged must go away, because of reports of serious anti-foreign action on the part of the revolutionists. They were very near then, those armies. One could, if one listened, hear the sound of distant cannon. And the final contingent of those white people who had decided to leave were going that day. It was the last chance, and if it were refused, there would be no other. All who stayed must stay through to whatever the end would be, because the crisis of battle was near, and the great city gates would be locked, and none could go out or come in until it was known who were the victors.

Carie's daughter took thought that morning. She believed in the revolutionists, but there might be a rabble after the battle. She thought of her small children, of her sister who had taken refuge with her from a city in the far interior already held by the revolutionists—that narrow escape had not been very promising. And there was her sister's child, too. Well, they could manage with the children, but what of Andrew? He could not walk far or endure hardship any more now. She begged him to go to certain safety.

But Andrew when compelled against his will had a trick of falling ill. It was not conscious pretense—it was an actual disturbance caused by the distress of not having his own way. When she went upstairs to call him to get ready to go he lay there on that narrow iron bed of his, the sheet pulled up to his chin.

"I'm ill," he said very faintly. "I couldn't possibly go."

She looked at him, knowing him, and that there was no persuading him.

"Then we all stay together," she said, and went away and closed the door.

Through that whole day the sound of the guns grew louder and the echo more hard against the rocks of the mountain. By afternoon the city gates were already locked, and there was a strange tense stillness everywhere. Shops were closed, and the streets were empty. People sat behind closed doors, waiting for no one knew what. They had done the same thing many times before, and even the children had been through wars. But this time it was different. One heard such things—the laborers, servants, apprentices, the poor who lived in the mud huts—they were all full of a strange excitement. No one knew what to expect.

In the empty streets Andrew's rickshaw passed as usual, his puller trotting along in the old frock coat. It was March and the air was still keen. Andrew preached that night in one of his street chapels, but almost no one was there to hear him and those who were hurried away quickly into the darkness. He came home to find the whole house alight and a steady stream of Chinese neighbors pouring into the gates. The cellars were full of unknown and poor people taking refuge. It had always been safe in the foreigners' houses before. In no war since 1900 had the foreigners been attacked—the foreigners had gunboats and treaties to take care of them. It was all familiar enough to Andrew. He sat in the living-room with the family and their Chinese friends. Only the unknowing children were asleep.

"This floor seems to seethe," he said. "The cellars are so full." Then he said, "I'm glad I stayed. One must share the life of those one has chosen to be one's own people."

Midnight came on and still there was no news and nothing could be seen in the darkness, and there was only the constant roaring of cannon to be heard. He was very tired. "Since I can't settle any of the fighting, I think I'll go to bed," he said at last with his dry smile. And so he went upstairs to lie and listen to the cracking guns. Near dawn there was a sudden silence and before he could wonder what it was he fell asleep.

It seemed no different from other days, that revolutionary dawn. He woke and the March sun filled his room, and from downstairs came the clatter of breakfast dishes and the smell of bacon and coffee. There were no more guns. Everything was over. He did not need to miss a single day of work. He got up, bathed in the shower he had rigged up for himself out of a small tin tub and the nozzle of a flower sprinkler, and dressed carefully and went downstairs, very cheerful and triumphant, to the usual seven o'clock breakfast. They were all waiting for him, children and grandchildren, and Carie's daughter was gay over the first daffodils of spring from her garden. She had run out before breakfast and cut them and they were on the table.

"Prophetic daffodils!" she said. "I'm glad they waited to open until today."

Everything was all right, they said. The revolutionists

had won, the city gates were open, the city had surrendered and was quiet. The Chinese had all gone home to breakfast, and the house was normal again.

"How silly to have gone away!" they told each other over bacon and eggs.

"Wars are all about the same in my experience," said Andrew in great content.

It was a cheerful meal, and afterwards the men hurried off to eight o'clock classes, and Carie's daughter tucked Andrew's lap robe about him in his rickshaw and put a small red rosebud she had grown in a window pot into his buttonhole. Red was for the new day.

He could choose the road through the city or the back road through the hills. This morning he chose the hill road. The air was fresh and sharp and sweet, and the sunshine was warming.

But he had scarcely set himself to enjoy it when he heard his name shouted loudly, over and over. He looked about, but no one was near. Indeed, when he came to think of it, he had seen no one upon the road. Usually it was busy with farmers carrying their baskets of early fresh vegetables on their shoulders to the city markets, or the road was dusty with the feet of donkeys, carrying bags of rice crossed upon their backs. There had been no one.

Then he saw one of the servants from the house running after him, shouting to him. The rickshaw puller halted and the man came up panting. He was the color of cheese and his mouth was so dry he could scarcely speak.

"Old Teacher—Old Teacher—come back!" he panted. "They are killing the foreigners!"

"I don't believe it," said Andrew.

"It is true. One of them is dead already. They shot him in the street. Your elder daughter beseeches you to return."

"I won't," said Andrew. "I have work waiting for me. Go on!" he said to the puller, but the servant laid hands on the shafts.

"She said if you would not come I was to lift you and carry you back, though you struck me for it."

"As for me," said the puller. "I will not pull you on and have your blood on my body."

They had him helpless.

"Go back, then," said Andrew grimly.

It was not the first time he had had to think of being killed. The sunshine was grey to him. No one knew what this day would be—perhaps the end—and his work was not done.

When he reached the house they were gathered on the doorstep waiting for him. They had run out of the house just as they were, without coats and hats. In ten minutes the whole world had changed. The gayety of the breakfast table, the warm security of the house, were now as though they never had been.

"Here he is!" the servant shouted, and the puller lowered the shafts and he stepped out.

"What does all this mean?" he demanded.

"We must hide!" Carie's daughter cried to him.

Hide! All these little children! Besides, he hated the thought of it.

"We'd better go decently into the house and pray," he said.

"We can't delay," she replied. "The revolutionary armies are against us. They've killed the two Catholic fathers already, and Jack Williams!"

Before he could argue with her the servants came wailing and running toward them, and there were neighbors slipping in at the gate secretly.

"Hide—hide!" they begged him. "The foreigners' houses are no safety today."

"Where can we hide?" Carie's daughter cried.

The Chinese looked at each other. Who indeed dared to take the burden of these white people? If they were found in a man's house he would be killed and all his children. There was no use to die foolishly.

All the time a strange horrible uproar had been gathering out of the streets. It was the sound of a mob. There was no time to be lost. But there was nowhere to go. The white people looked at each other. This land had been home to them, for Andrew since his youth, for his children and their children since they were born. But suddenly, in an hour, it was home no more. Their house could not shelter them, no gates, no walls could make them safe.

A small stumpy blue-clad figure came running in the back gate as fast as her bound feet would let her. It was only a woman, a common peasant woman whom Carie's daughter had given food in a famine in the north country, and who in another famine had come south to find her again. Carie's daughter had not rejoiced to see the woman, penniless, half-starved and pregnant. But she took her in because she had a silly soft heart, and she let the baby boy be born there and took care of him to keep him from the tetanus by which the woman had lost every other child she had, and took care of him again when the woman once let him get nearly burned to death. She had not been at all pleased to do it, and had scolded the stupid grateful mother for her stupidity, and when the woman's husband wandered down from the north to hunt his wife she had been thankful to find him a job as a farm laborer and so get them all off her hands. But the baby grew into a chubby brown little boy, and it was nice to see him alive.

This woman, then, came running in. Her husband was away all day, and her little room empty, she said, and Carie's daughter and all her family were to come and hide there. It was only half a tiny hut, really, and no one would think of looking among mud huts. She was tugging at them, she had Carie's daughter's hand, and she pulled Andrew's sleeve, and picked up the smallest yellow-haired child, and started out of the gate and across the fields, and so they followed her.

In the packed silence of the tiny hut they sat down, some on the board bed, some on a bench, and she shut the door silently.

"This is a safe place," she whispered through the cracks. "There are so many children in these huts that if a little foreign child cries it will not be known."

But none of the little foreign children cried that livelong day. There were two little girls and a little boy, none of them yet five years old, a lively, noisy trio on other days. Today, in the darkness, in the strange howling roar outside, they sat perfectly still upon their elders' knees, knowing somehow in what peril they were.

As for Andrew, he could not believe this was the end. All day he sat without a word, among his children and grandchildren. But no one spoke. Each of them was busy in himself. Andrew was thinking back over the years. "Not so much thinking," he wrote afterwards, "as letting the pictures of what had gone drift across my mind. Often I thought I was somewhere else." And one of Carie's daughters sat thinking of her unborn child and wondering if he would now live to be born. And the other sat looking at her two little girls and thought steadfastly how when the hour came she must be strong and before she died herself she must see them dead first, though she did it herself, and not leave them in the hands of the soldiers.

The strange hours passed. The servants stole across the fields with loaves of bread under their coats and a bottle of boiled water and a tin of milk for the children. Every now and again the door opened and the face of a Chinese friend would appear. Only there was always that moment of fear—was he a friend? Who could tell in this day? But they were friends, and they came in to knock their heads before us, and to beg us to take heart because they were doing all they could with the revolutionary leaders to intercede with them for our lives. And at noon the door opened again and a kind unknown motherly Chinese woman came in with bowls of hot rice gruel and told us to eat and not fear—that no one in all the little cluster of huts would tell that we were there. They had threatened even their children, she said. "I told my little devil I would beat him to death if he told," she said to comfort us. And the day mounted to noon.

The noise outside the hut increased. Andrew had heard that noise before—the noise not of angry people but of people in greed, of poor people who see what they have coveted now within reach. There was the sound of thudding upon wood, of a gate being crashed in, the sounds of feet running across ground, of wooden doors splintering, and then the howling of greed again.

"They've got in the house," said Andrew suddenly.

The hut door opened as he spoke and the two Chinese came in who had been interceding with the revolutionary leaders. They fell on the earthen floor before Andrew.

"Forgive us," they said, "we cannot save your lives. We have done all we can, but there is no longer hope."

And rising and bowing, they went away, their faces the color of clay.

For two hours Andrew and his children sat waiting, expecting every instant to see the door open and soldiers rush in. But it did not open. And outside the din went on, the shouting and the howling. The hut was lit with firelight now—they were burning the foreigners' houses. There could be only a few minutes left. Each in his own fashion took leave of life and earth and thought of how to die proudly before an enemy race, and Andrew bowed his head. The children were asleep in our arms, heartbreakingly precious because it was the last time. The next moment—in an hour at most—it would be finished for us all.

Then across the horror and the din there came a terrific thunder. The hut shook and the children woke. Again it came, again and again, such thunder as none of us had ever heard before. Our ears were stopped with the noise.

We stared at each other, asking—it was not thunder from heaven—not this regular repeated roar.

"Cannon!" cried one of the men.

Andrew shook his head. "The Chinese have no such cannon," he shouted above the din.

"American—British cannon," the other shouted back.

Then we remembered what we had all forgotten—there were American, English and Japanese gunboats in the river seven miles away. They had opened fire on the city. We were in a fresh danger. We might be blown to pieces by our own guns. But instantly we were all relieved—it would at least be a clean death, quick and clean—no torture at the hands of Chinese soldiers.

Suddenly it was over. All noise ceased. The guns stopped, and there was silence, a strange, sudden complete silence. There was no more sound of shouting, no more howling, no more screeching of wrenched and breaking wood. Only the sound of crackling flames went on and the dark little hut was brighter than any day could light it.

Andrew stood up and looked through the tiny window and across the hills. He pressed his face against the hole, staring at something.

"They are burning the seminary buildings!" he whispered. And he sat down and covered his eyes with his hand. His work was gone again. . . .

There was nothing to do but wait now. Someone would come and tell us what to do. It was a long and dreary waiting, the hardest of the day. None of us could guess what the bombardment meant or what the silence. Was the city laid waste under those mighty guns and were we only left alive? No one came near.

Late that night the door opened. There stood two of our Chinese friends, with a guard of soldiers.

"We have come to take you to a safe place," they said gladly.

But the soldiers made us halt. They were in a strange uniform and surely there never was so villainous a guard. Their faces were jeering and flushed, and their features swollen as though they were drunken. They stood there, leaning on their guns, the light of the torches on their wicked, mocking faces. We shrank back. Commit the children and Andrew to these?

"But these are the same soldiers who have been attacking us all day," Carie's daughter protested.

But there was no other way.

"It is your only chance," our friends urged us. "All the white people are gathered in the big laboratory in the university. We will take you there."

So one by one, Andrew first, we filed out of the tiny hut, eight feet by ten, where we had lived for thirteen hours, three men, two women and the three little children. Those three great tall men! Carie's daughter never thought them so huge before that day.

Across the dark fields we went, past smoking and charred ruins of what only that morning had been cheerful American homes, to the black pile of the university buildings. Once a little weary child, stumbling, fell against a soldier and he turned with a snarl that made the heart stop. But the child's mother cried out, "She did not mean to push you—she is only three years old!" and the soldier went on with a grunt.

So at last we reached the gate of the university. There stood another guard of revolutionary soldiers, the same dark, jeering, evil-looking men. They laughed as we came by and seized their guns and shook them to frighten us. But not even a child cried—they only looked, wondering, having been taught all their small lives to like the Chinese and call them friends. So the dreary little procession entered the building and filed upstairs in the darkness.

There in the big laboratory we found gathered over a hundred white people, men, women, and children, nearly all Americans. Seven had been killed since dawn, but all these others had hidden somehow and been hidden by Chinese friends, and had been rescued after much hideous experience at the hands of mobs and soldiers. We had been very fortunate, we found afterwards. Few of the other white people had not had to face their enemies in one way or another. But the dreadful day was over, and now the darkness covered them and they were trying to rest. Yet at every fresh entrance they cried out to know who was there and if they were safe. One by one, all through the restless night, the white people came in, some wounded, some beaten, but no more dead. But no one knew what the dawn would be, for the city belonged to the revolution now.

All through the next day we waited, gathered together in the big room. It was not a sad day, though no one knew what its end might be. We organized ourselves, distributed what food there was, and attended to those who were ill and wounded or had newborn babies. And there were those Chinese working for us. They came and went, bringing food and clothes and bedding. They came weeping and begging forgiveness, and telling us that the dead were decently buried. They brought us toothbrushes and towels and coats, for the March wind was piercingly cold and the buildings were unheated, and the soldiers had robbed us of warm outer garments.

All of us were homeless and penniless, and we did not know whether or not we were yet to be massacred, and there were among us the widowed and those young mothers of newly born babies and women who had suffered such indignity at the hands of mad soldiery as cannot be told. But somehow the day was not sad. We were not friendless. There was not one of us who had not friends among the Chinese and these risked their lives to bring us comfort. For after we went, if ever we were to go, their names would be upon a proscribed list of those who had helped foreigners, and who were "running dogs of the imperialists."

In the afternoon the order came from the guard for us to move out, and go down to the bund seven miles away and get on the American and English battleships in the harbor. We were hurried out by the same wicked-looking soldiers into the street and in broken-down carriages, or on foot or however we could, the march began. At dusk we rounded the road to the river and there, alight from stem to stern, the battleships lay waiting. American marines, American sailor boys, were standing on the bund and they hurried forward and helped old men and women and children into the dories, and then there was the rush of the dark water about the boats, the heave and sweep of the swelling current, the black precipice of the ship's side and the swinging ladderway, and at last the firm deck beneath the feet. Hearty voices cried out, "You're on American territory now—cheer up!" "Supper's waitin'!"

But it was all a daze—the crowded cabins, the small saloon, the pots of hot food on the table, soup and baked beans and stew, ladled out by shouting, joking sailors. Food and sleep—and oh, the heaven of safety! Women who had not wept once, who had stood up to pillage and cruelty and death, could not keep from weeping, and brave little children who had stood straight and defiant beside their parents before the guns of the soldiers, cried endlessly about nothing.

As for Andrew, he disappeared from the table and Carie's daughter went out to find him and see how he did. He was standing by the ship's side, staring across the water to the dark city. There was not a light in it, but he knew where it lay, for dim against the sky he could see the crest of the mountain, and the city walls curled about the mountain's foot.

"What are you thinking?" she asked.

"I was just planning about going back," he said quietly. He did not turn or say anything more, and she left him there, gazing into the dark city. Going back! Of course he would be thinking of nothing else.

It is hard to separate one thing from another now. It is all a jumble of faces and stories, tears and laughter. Everyone on the ships had a story, a miracle to tell, now that all were safe. An old American whose hobby was honey-making told of a greedy soldier who thought his hives held treasure and opened one rudely and was set upon by furious bees and ran howling across the garden. A doctor, caught in his hospital, covered his face and hands with scarlet mercurochrome and pretended to be mad when the soldiers came and they ran from him. Another, a doctor from a southern state, hid in his own coal cellar all day, and when he was rescued, marched into the laboratory, his face black with soot, declaring grimly to his fellows, "I'm going home—this is no country for a white man!" and wondered why the others laughed, starving and desperate as they were. There was the wife who swallowed her wedding ring to save it from the greedy clutching hands of the soldiers, and wore it again, triumphantly, the last day upon the battleship.

But there were other stories not for laughter—an old lady who stood immobile while the soldiers jerked at her wedding ring and diamond solitaire, and when one pulled his sword to cut off her finger, remarked in calm English, "You'll not get it off otherwise, my man—it's been on for fifty years." And there was the story of a Chinese professor at his watch at the telephone in the university just before dawn who might have saved us all. The night before the battle had been divided into watches, for it had been arranged that when the revolutionary armies entered the south gate outside which the battle was fought, it should be telephoned to the university, at the north side, what their temper was. There was no other telephone in that end of the city, and the news was then to be taken by foot to each house. But the Chinese professor, though trained at the best American schools of agriculture and forestry, was fat and lazy, and he laid himself down and slept, not believing, to do him justice, that anything would happen. The telephone rang and rang, but he slept. Had he waked or been at his post, some would have been alive today who are dead, and many would have been spared hours which they dare not remember.

Into Shanghai they poured, these worn creatures, to find what shelter they could. Most of them were too sad and disheartened to do anything else than buy tickets on the first boat home, never to return to China.

But Andrew had his plans all made. He said briskly, "I've always heard that the mission work in Korea is so much more successful than in China, and I've always wanted to see why. I'm going to Korea."

"Not by yourself!" Carie's daughter exclaimed.

"All by myself," he said firmly, and went.

What he did in Korea could only be gathered from his scanty letters. He managed somehow to get about a great deal. He discovered colonies of Chinese in Korea who had no churches, since the missionaries in Korea spoke no Chinese, and so immediately he began preaching to them, holding services in their homes, and working to organize them into a church. His letters grew buoyant at once and enthusiastic as though nothing had happened to him. "It's extraordinary," he wrote, "how the work lies waiting to be done."

"The Chinese," he wrote again, "are worth much more than these Koreans. Even here it is the Chinese who do the work and carry on the business. So far as I can see the Korean men do nothing but sit about in their white dresses and get dirty, and the women do nothing but wash the dresses."

He grew immensely scornful of the Korean dress. "No people can amount to anything who wear such silly clothes," he wrote. "The men wear white linen skirts and little tall hats tied under their chins. Their souls seem scarcely worth saving."

"If the Japanese were not here," he wrote again, "I do not believe the Koreans would trouble even to feed themselves."

He came back after six months, in good health and perfectly complacent.

"It is no wonder the missionaries in Korea have such an easy time," he declared. "Anybody can convert a Korean. It's as hard to convert one Chinese as it is twenty Koreans, but you have more in the end. Now I'm going back to real work."

None of us could dissuade him, not even a threatening consul. No one of the Americans had been allowed to return to Nanking except a few young men on occasional visits of supervision. There were no decent places to live. Such foreign houses as had not been destroyed were filled with soldiers. Everything was disorganized and the anti-foreign feeling was still high.

But Andrew pshawed at everything. His trip to the

cooler climate of Korea had done him good, and he was full of his high serene obstinacy.

"I don't want a house," he said. "I'll get a room somewhere, and a boy to cook rice and eggs. I don't need any more."

There was nothing to be done with him—there never had been. Carie's daughter, scolding him heartily, packed his small bag and slipped in all the extras she could, without any hope that he would ever use them. And she sent for a faithful servant and bade him go with the old son of God and serve him and watch over him, and so they went off, she half believing she would never see Andrew again. There were terrible tales of cholera and typhus and dysentery that year. And only the very poor were eating the crabs that dug into the banks of the river and canals. Crabs were usually dear and a delicacy for the rich, but this year, though they had never been so fat, the rich were too dainty to eat them because there had been so many dead thrown into the waters, so the poor feasted for once.

But nothing stopped Andrew from what he wanted to do. His man found him a wretched little room in a half-ruined school building and bought a clay charcoal stove the size of a bucket and an earthen pot, and Andrew bought an old iron cot and a chair and a table—foreign stuff sold cheaply these days, and second-hand shops were full of loot—and so he was at work again. The seminary buildings were nearly all burned, and what was left of them was occupied by some war lord general or other who had for the time being thrown in his lot with the revolution. It was years before they were given back.

But Andrew never believed much in buildings anyway. He began looking about for the students and he found them here and there. People told him tales about these divinity students. There had been communists among them, and these had led mobs against the foreigners. But Andrew was not troubled.

"I don't believe it," he said serenely, and would not.

He liked being the only white man back. "It's perfectly safe—all nonsense those consuls talk," he wrote to Carie's daughter. He enjoyed his life those days. And the people along the streets, small shopkeepers and the lords of little inns, and poor people of all sorts called out after him and laughed to see him and were glad to have him back. "Well, it is the Old Teacher back again!" "The Old Teacher has more courage than any of them!" "Stop and drink a bowl of tea, Old Teacher!" they shouted as he passed in his rickshaw.

He loved their welcome and their admiration, and he was living the life of poverty he liked to live. He promptly began to preach on the streets and in the tea shops, and at a time when no other white man could find a house or a room, because no one wanted to rent to foreigners,

Andrew somehow rented two different rooms opening on busy streets, bought some benches and two pulpits looted from other churches before the revolution, and was preaching every day and again at night. One of the pulpits was out of the Methodist church and Andrew took a satisfaction in that. "Sound doctrine coming from behind it now!" he said with his dry smile.

And people came to hear him, people who were already beginning to be disillusioned with the revolutionists and their vast promises never redeemed. Disgruntled laborers muttered, "They said we would all have good jobs in factories and they gave us little tickets to prove we were to have a job. 'Show the ticket at the gate,' they said. What gate—what factory? They were dreams!"

Now and again a young student communist would break up a meeting, but Andrew only said mildly to the dispersing crowd, "We will meet again tomorrow as usual at the same hour," and no one could outdo that immense determination. So at a time when no one else could work among the people, he worked in his usual way, without fear or haste.

The outward circumstances of life, indeed, meant nothing to him—a house, a home, food, comfort, all were nothing. His home was in his work, his heart to do God's business. There was no other happiness for him.

When Carie's daughter came back after a year away and set herself to the making again of a home out of a ruined house, defiled by filth and used as a cholera base for months, she found Andrew very serene and quiet. Indeed he seemed scarcely of earth at all any more, so bodiless had he grown, living alone, speaking little except to preach, eating his too frugal food. The faithful manservant grieved and complained to Carie's daughter that Andrew ate almost nothing.

"His heart is too hot for an old man," the servant mourned. "He burns from within."

She prepared his room first as she knew he liked it and moved him into it without disturbance to him, and he scarcely realized the change. He seemed to have forgotten there had ever been a revolution.

XII

HE grew very gentle as months went on into a year. All the old high energy went away from him, and he was always gentle. He was not so critical, either, as once he was, nor did he distinguish so hardly as once he had between other creeds and his own. He disliked denominationalism more than ever, but in these days he even could forgive a man for believing in immersion, and he did not argue any more over anything. His own belief was unshakeable. He believed word for word in the Apostles' Creed, and he lived happily in the full confidence of the second coming of Jesus Christ. One day Christ would appear in the sky, it was sure to him, and the bodies of the righteous would rise from the dead and be caught up with Christ. But Andrew did not wait in anxiety for this coming. He hoped not to die—at the word death that terror crept into his eyes and caught at the heart of Carie's daughter—but he said quite tranquilly, "We are not told when Christ shall appear—it may be tomorrow, it may be in a thousand years."

But he rather thought it would not be a thousand years. He used to tell Carie's daughter there were certain signs—wars and famines and distress, and especially the rising of what he called "anti-Christ" in Russia. Carie's daughter listened and never argued with him, or ever showed her unbelief. Not for her life would she have robbed Andrew of one atom of that faith which had made life so worth living to him, not now when he was old and needed the faith by which to die. And he never thought to ask her what her own faith was, being so full of his own.

So he lived his last few mellow golden years, never crossed, and humored in all ways, both large and small. So unhindered, he seemed to turn before our eyes into a gentle spirit, more frugal of food and drink than ever, more quiet in speech, more transcendent, more remote from earth.

When the perception of the dissolution of his life came to him it is hard to tell. But to him, as to all old, there came gradually the knowledge that there were not many more days in which to work, not many nights left in which to lie down to sleep, and there would soon be a dawn to which he would not wake. Sometimes at twilight he would seem timorous of being alone, as though he remembered the old ghost stories he had heard as a child. He wanted the lights early, and he wanted to hear human voices, to have people about him. Carie's daughter stayed near then, and spoke to him cheerfully of small things, and sat by him with everyday sewing in her hands, and encouraged the children to run in and out. He was comforted by such small ways, and warmed, though he never knew how to share in the life of home or children. But he sat and watched and the look of fear went out of his eyes and after a while he could go up to bed. And Carie's daughter always made a pretext to go up to his room on such nights and see that his blanket was tucked in about him warmly and that the light was ready for his touch and she put on the table by him a little bell to call her in the night, and she left the door open a crack so that he could hear the footsteps in the house and not lie alone thinking of the past gone and death soon ahead.

When dawn came and brought his work he was himself again. Nothing could keep him from his work, nor would Carie's daughter hold him back, knowing that to let him go was life and strength to him.

But in the spring of his eightieth year even his work began to be too much. There was a change that year. His flesh grew almost transparent, until his body looked like a pale mist, like a pure wraith, out of which his eyes shone luminous with disembodied goodness. Everything human had gone from him, all appetite, all anger, all impetuosity. Even the old stubbornness was gone. Much of the time after he had come slowly home from work he spent lying down, his eyes closed. But he liked to lie in the room where Carie's daughter was. Sometimes when she looked up from her work he would be lying there on the sofa, so white, so still, that she would cry out. Then he would open his eyes.

"I'm quite all right," he would say. "I've had a good day's work and I'm resting now."

Yes, there was a change that spring. The early April warmth did not stir him, and for the first time he did not look with longing to the hills. Carie's daughter grew afraid and called a doctor, and the doctor said, "Nothing wrong—just worn out—let him have his way in everything." He always had.

The end came happily and quickly that summer. The heat had made him very faint, and so quite willingly he agreed to go up the river to the Lu Shan mountains to his other daughter. He went off happily with his son-in-law, who came to fetch him. He was feeling well that day and he made small jokes as he went. And they wrote back that the journey seemed to revive him, and in the mountain air he was more himself than he had been for a long time.

All that summer he was happy. He met old friends, and enemies so old that they seemed friends at last, and they forgot old quarrels and made much of him, and his daughter planned little pleasures for him. The summer passed quickly and suddenly he was, he said, ready for work again. He was better—he had played too long—he had not had such a holiday in years. So he wrote to Carie's daughter and she prepared his room and made it all fresh and ready, and waited for him.

That was the summer of the torrential Yangtse flood.

The telegraph poles along the river were torn out by the roots and swirled down to the ocean, and steamers with mails were delayed for days. When Andrew, too, was delayed, she did not worry greatly. No one was getting through. Then, after a week, a letter came through and a telegram, relayed somehow by devious lines. Andrew was gone. There on the mountain top he had been taken ill one night with his old dysentery and in a few short hours it was over. There had been not much pain, not much suffering, only a deep bodily weakness, out of which his spirit broke with a great groan, gladly, into its own freedom.

But the body was so little a part of him that its final stillness seemed nothing of importance. He was half out of it anyway and death was only a slipping out of it altogether and being at last what he always was, a spirit. We buried the pearly shell upon the mountain top. There is nothing between that spot and the sky—no tree, no human habitation. The rocks are beneath, the swirling mists about it, and the winds blow and the sun and the stars shine down, and there is no human voice to be heard anywhere.

It is the unfathomed irony of all life, now, to think, years past, that Carie who loved the height of clean high mountains and longed to live up and upon them, body and soul, should lie forever buried in a hot dark place, in a parcel of ground walled about in the heart of a Chinese city to hold a few foreign dead. The very air where she lies is full of human miasma, and about her is the ceaseless roar of human shouting and quarreling and laughter and wailing. The high walls and the locked gates cannot hold them from her even now. And Andrew, who sought men for their souls, lies lonely and free upon his mountain top, as far from her in death as life had made him. She longed all her life to be out of human hold and heat, and all her life humanity held her prisoner, her own humanity and that of all the world, and death was a battle with life and she lost. But Andrew never touched the fringe of human life, he never knew its stuff, he never felt its doubt nor shared its pain. And so he lived, a happy soul, and never knew he died.